GW00762066

Best of Irish Poetry
Scoth na hÉigse

2007

Colm Breathnach, Eagarthóir
Maurice Riordan, Editor

SOUTHWORDeditions

First published in 2006
by Southword Editions,
the Munster Literature Centre,
Frank O'Connor House, 84 Douglas Street,
Cork, Ireland.

www.munsterlit.ie

ISBN-10: 1-905002-23-8
ISBN-13: 9781-905002-23-8

Contents

Réamhrá

Is é a chuireas romham a dhéanamh anseo an deich ndán Gaeilge is fearr dar liom a foilsíodh i gcaitheamh na tréimhse a leagadh síos don díolaim, ó Lúnasa 2005 go deireadh mhí Iúil 2006, a bhailiú le chéile. Is é sin dánta a foilsíodh den chéad uair i gcaitheamh na tréimhse sin. Ní raibh sé i gceist agam blaiseadh a thabhairt dá bhfuil á scríobh i gcoitinne faoi láthair ná iarracht a dhéanamh, ach chomh beag, stíleanna éagsúla na filíochta reatha, más ann dá leithéid, a léiriú. *Scoth na héigse* le linn na tréimhse úd, sin a raibh i gceist. Tugann an saothar ealaíne sinn i láthair, is é sin inár láthair féin nó i láthair an duine eile ar shlí gur féidir linn an mothú nó an machnamh nó an mhóimint is ócáid don saothar a bhrath. Déanann an dán maith an méid sin, ní tríd an ócáid a thuairisciú, ach tríd an ócáid a chruthú ar phár le fuinneamh an fhriotail a úsáidtear agus trí ghuth sainiúil an fhile. Cuirtear léas nó tuiscint nó braistint ar leith an fhile ar fáil dúinn trí na focail a roghnaítear agus na nathanna a chumtar agus trí struchtúr nó foirm an dáin. Téann na nithe sin i bhfeidhm ar gach léitheoir ar shlite éagsúla agus mar sin ní féidir ach gur rogha phearsanta a bheidh in aon rogha mar seo a dhéanfar. Sa chás seo is filí go bhfuil go leor curtha i gcrích acu cheana féin don gcuid is mó atá roghnaithe. Filí iad atá ag saothrú na filíochta le tamall agus a rian sin ar na dánta leo atá anseo. Ceardaithe iad a bhíonn i láthair tráth na hinspioráide.

Bhí an dán 'Déirc' le Michael Davitt léite agam sara bhfaca mé foilsithe é agus nuair d'aimsigh mé i gcló é ba é an chéad dán é a roghnaíos le haghaidh na díolama seo. Is é an dán deireanach é a scríobh Michael agus mar sin is dóigh liom go bhfuil sé oiriúnach go mbeadh sé sa chéad eagrán seo de *Scoth na hÉigse*. Agus is dán Davittiúil é, dar ndóigh. Tá an fonn agus an fiafraí ba ghnách leis ar fáil anseo. An fonn chun na beatha agus an fiafraí sin a dheineadh sé agus an scagadh i dtaobh a mheoin fhéin i leith an tsaoil. Tá an méid sin ann agus an bháidh nádúrtha chineálta a bhí aige le daoine. Amuigh ag siúl faoin dtuath sa Ghascóin, mar a rabhadar ag cur fúthu an tráth úd, atá an file agus a pháirtí, iad ag iarraidh dul amach ar an ndúthaigh agus aithne a chur ar mhuintir na háite, is dócha. Le linn dóibh stopadh ag tigh le deoch uisce a

9

lorg chun an spalladh atá orthu a mhúchadh tugtar ar ais an file ina chuimhne go dtí a óige agus an tráth a bhíodh lucht déirce ag teacht chun an tí ag baile. An léim Dhavittiúil sin in aon líne amháin ón iarraidh a dhéanann siad ar an tseana-bhean ("de dhéine shéimh Pheig Sayers") i bhFraincis thámáilte, "An mbeadh *un verre d'eau* aici?", go dtí an freagra a chuirtear in iúl i nGaeilge, mar dhea is gurb í Fraincis thíriúil na mná tí í, "Bheadh agus bucaod", is í an léim sin a thugann siar sinn ón tsiúlóid seo sa bhFrainc go dtí an "déircínteacht fadó". Sa chnuasach *Seimeing Soir*, thug Michael "Múscraí Uí Fhloinn na Fraince" ar an nGascóin agus seo é arís, sa dán atá anseo againn, ag athghabháil mheon sin an tsaoil mar a bhí agus é óg, é ina scoláire i gColáiste na Gascóine mar a déarfá ag foghlaim go mb'fhéidir gur leor "bheith i láthair in am an ghátair". Is gur buaine binne an tráth sin an teangmháil dhaonna ná an déirc a bhronntar.

Is minic i bhfilíocht Biddy Jenkinson pearsana ón seanchas ag eitilt tríd an spéir agus ag tuirlingt i gcrainn. Sa chás seo, in 'Guthanna Sinseartha', taibhsí a mamó agus sean-aintín léi atá "suite i dtom aitinn" ag áiteamh fheidhm na haithne Béarla '*Cast not a clout till May is out*' uirthi nuair a chaitheann sí di a cóta agus í ag garraíodóireacht Lá Bealtaine mar gur "lá bog tais" é agus "ceobhrán allasach báistí anuas". Luann an file gurb é is brí le "May" an Bhéarla sa nath ná "bláth na sceiche gile" a sceitheann i lár na Bealtaine seachas ainm na míosa. Luann sí, leis, go mbaineann an nath leis an ré sarar athraíodh an féilire faoin bPápa Gréagóir agus mar sin gurb é tús mhí na Bealtaine seachas a deireadh an tráth go bhfuil tagairt dó sa nath ó cheart. Cuimhníonn an file ar na blianta go léir a d'fhulaing sí:

...an veist gheimhridh
a chuirtí orm, im leanbh, ag tús na Samhna
mar d'ordaigh Dia, cosaint ar an eitinn
— cniotáilte de bháinín oíliúil garbh —
le cneas,
go deireadh Bhealtaine...
'...*till May is out!*'

Cúram file focail agus anseo léirítear an tslí ina leanann focail d'intinn an fhile agus féach freisin gur i dtéarmaí focal a chuirtear an tseana-choimhlint idir an duine aonair agus an traidisiún dochumhscaithe i láthair. Níl na húdair Bhéarla ar aon fhocal i dtaobh brí an fhocail "may" sa seanrá sin agus féach, ainneoin a deir an file, gur ceannlitir atá leis an bhfocal aici tríd síos sa dán nó lena chur ar shlí eile:

Labhraíonn taibhsí
ach ní éisteann siad linn.

Bímid go léir óg i láthair ghuthanna na sinsear, ag cur na gcos uainn, ag iarraidh cur ina gcoinne pé slí is féidir linn agus an-léiriú air sin atá tugtha dúinn sa dán seo.

Tá an dán 'Fuascailt' le Dairena Ní Chinnéide le fáil sa chéad chnuasach uaithi *An Trodaí agus dánta eile* gur céadchnuasach suaithinseach fórsúil é. Cuirtear an carachtar mná seo an Trodaí i láthair i sraith dánta i ndeireadh an chnuasaigh. Bean í a ghluaiseann sna dánta sin idir saol leathdhraíochtúil nó miotasach in Iarthar Duibhneach agus áiteanna mar "Ghleann an gCrann", in éineacht le neacha eile mar "an sealgaire" agus "an mac tíre", ar thaobh amháin agus an gnáthshaol i dtigh leathscoite nó ar thuras go Corcaigh ar an dtaobh eile. Níorbh fhéidir dar liom dán a roghnú as sraith dánta le haghaidh na díolama seo mar is dóigh liom go mbaineann an éifeacht atá leo, cuid mhaith, leis an tslí ina gcuireann na dánta le chéile chun aonad iomlán a chruthú. Tá an mianach céanna, áfach, sa dán 'Fuascailt' is atá sna dánta sa tsraith 'An Trodaí' ach amháin go seasann an dán seo leis féin. Tá an dá shnáithe ag sní tríd an dán. Tá ceiliúradh agus caoineadh araon ann. Léirítear neart agus laige na pearsan, rud a dheineann bean iomlán den mbean a chuirtear os á gcomhair. Gluaiseann an dán ó ghníomh athshlánaitheach grá go luaitear "fuascailt anama" leis go dtí cuimhne ar eachtra choscrach collaí "a d'fháisc sí ina haigne feadh a saoil" agus amach as arís. Labhraítear go hoscailte agus go folaitheach sa dán. Tá caint dhíreach ann mar "Seacht masla agus maisle ort, a fhir,/A shanntaigh cuid colainne do chomharsan" agus claontagairtí mar "Do leath an ghrian ag a cosa/Do chuala sí cantan na manach". Is é an teannas défhiúsach sin sa dán agus sa ghuth a labhraíonn linn tríd an ndán, ag luascadh dó ó neart go laige, ón ngrá go dtí an ghráin, a fhágann gur ráiteas láidir é an dán seo.

Ainneoin na foirme, dán gruama is ea 'Muisiriún' le Nuala Ní Dhomhnaill. Cuireann an rithim agus na línte gearra seolta i gcéill gur dán éadrom é ach, diaidh ar ndiaidh, de réir mar a leantar de thréithe agus de mhianach an mhuisiriúin a liostú, éiríonn a dán níos dorcha. Is dóigh liom gurb in príomhbhua an dáin, an tslí ina gclaochlaítear an fhoirm féin agus go ndéantar sraith ráiteas mailíseach binbeach bagarthach de na línte de réir a chéile. Tosnaítear le:

> Ba mhaith liom a bheith im mhuisiriún,
> óm bhaithis síos go dtí bundún...

línte atá páistiúil geall leis do, sa tslí gur deacair glacadh dáiríre leis an dá líne a leanann iad "im chlár nimhe, ag fógairt oilc,/ag bagairt báis do shlua an tsuilt". Ach faoi lár an dáin, tar éis "d'fhásfainn gan mhairg ar gach a d'éag", nuair a léimid:

> Nár lige Dia go mbainfir greim
> as an nathair bhreac, nó an púca peill,
> an balbhán béice, caidhp an bháis
> níl insint scéil ar an bpianpháis
>
> a leanann iad, an céasadh ceart.
> Níl leigheas le fáilt ná aon teacht as.
> Is bheinn go sásta ina measc
> ag ídiú saoil, ag scaipeadh báis.

níl aon amhras orainn a thuilleadh ach gur dán a fáisceadh as an duairceas an dán seo. Críochnaíonn an dán le ciúta beagnach meánaoiseach i dtaobh an bás a bheith i ndán do chách.

Lá éigin bead im mhuisiriún
ag sá trín gcré is trín gcomhrainn throm.
Is beidh mo lámha bána lách'
i ndán don duine seang is don sách.

Dán duairc é seo faoin mbás nó b'fhéidir díreach faoin nduairceas nó faoin ndubhachas nó faoin ngalar dubhach. Is é an smacht a choinnítear ar an bhfoirm agus an tslí ina mbogtar chun cinn de réir a chéile ó airíonna an mhuisiriúin féin i dtús an dáin go dtí an bhagairt ar deireadh a chuireann brí ann mar aiste.

Dán ciúin tomhaiste is ea 'An Bosca Seacláide' le hÁine Ní Ghlinn as an gcnuasach *Tostanna.* Cruthaítear an radharc diaidh ar ndiaidh ann de réir mar a fhéachann iníon tríd an méid stuif a bhí i dtaisce i mbosca seacláide ag a máthair a cailleadh agus atá díreach curtha aici. Gnáth-mhionbhlúirí páipéir srl. a bheadh á gcoimeád i mbosca mar sin, pátrúin chniotála, cártaí cuimh-neacháin, agus mar sin de, atá ann. Ach i bhfolach istigh faoin stuif seo tá beart grianghraf ina bhfuil:

...báibín, a raibh a súile féin aici,
cailín óg, déagóir, bean mheánaosta a d'aithin sí ach
fós nár aithin....

Tar éis féachaint ar na grianghraif seo agus ar a hathair atá ag "míogarnach cois tine" cuireann sí ar ais iad sa bhosca agus cuireann sí an ribín agus an "banda ruibéir" a bhí bainte den mbosca ar ais air agus cuireann sí an bosca ar ais ar an tseilf agus deir sí paidir "ar son anamacha na mbeo is na marbh". Gluaiseann an dán ó oscailt an bhosca go dúnadh an bhosca, i gcroí an dáin atá an buille, áfach, nuair a deirtear i dtaobh na ngrianghraf go bhfuil a "...rún féin á scaoileadh ag na dátaí/ar chúl gach uile cheann". Cruthaítear atmaisféar agus rithim thomhaiste leis an gcomhshondas atá coitianta tríd an gcéad chúpla véarsa agus leis an gcuntas tuairisciúil ar a raibh sa bhosca. Cuirtear tábhacht an rúin a bhaineann leis na grianghraif in iúl trí ghnáthúlacht na nithe eile a bhí sa bhosca ina dteannta. Agus faoi mar nach ligeann an bhean atá sa dán aon ní uirthi lena hathair, i ndeireadh an dáin fágtar a bpríobháideachas ag na ndaoine seo go bhfuaireamar an éachtaint seo orthu trí gan an rún féin a scaoileadh sa dán agus tríd an mbosca a dhúnadh agus a chur ar ais ar an tseilf arís.

Bhraitheas gur dán ar leith é 'Faoileoir' le Gréagóir Ó Dúill fiú agus é á léamh agam den gcéad uair agus teist mhaith ar dhán é sin. Radharc atá annamh ach simplí in éineacht atá i gceist sa dán. Agus an file ag tiomáint i dtreo na hairde ó thuaidh mar a bhfuil drochshíon ag bagairt sa spéir chíonn sé faoileoir ag briseadh amach as na scamaill agus ag casadh sa spéir ghlan agus "madaidh na stoirme sna sála air". Is é an cur i láthair simplí sofaisticiúil, áfach, seachas an radharc féin, a tharraingíonn an léitheoir leis, dar liom. Tá roinnt frásaí simplí tríd an téacs go bhfuil trombhrí leo mar gheall ar an áit ina dtiteann siad. "Tá seo le déanamh" a deir an file i dtreo dheireadh an chuir síos ar an dtiomáint ó thuaidh, macalla de "promises to keep" Robert Frost ann mar fhrása agus i dtreo dheireadh an chuir síos ar an bhfaoileoir, mar an gcéanna, tá "fear gan inneall". I gcás mo dhuine thíos "ní bhaineann toil le scéal", ní mór dó tiomáint – "tiomáint, sea leoga, tiomáint" – agus an fear thuas cé go bhfuil sé "gan talamh slán" fós is saoire é ná an fear thíos agus é:

...ag foluain ar tháirní creidimh
ag áinliú ar chleití na misní...

is cruthaíonn an chodarsnacht seo an dara leibhéal sa dán, ionas gur féidir é a léamh mar chur i láthair fisiciúil ar an mbunchoimhlint sin sa duine idir an dualgas nach mór a chomhlíonadh agus an tóir atá ann san am céanna ar shaoirse, ar "chiúnas beannaithe" b'fhéidir nó ar fhaill chun a chuartha féin a ghearradh ar "éadan na firmiminte", ar saoirse í nach féidir a bhaint amach, áfach, gan dul sa bhfiontar san "anfa doininne". Ní gá, dar ndóigh, an dara léamh sin a chur sa mheá in aon chor le taitneamh a bhaint as an dán. Tá an radharc chomh glé sin go bhfanann an pictiúr den bhfaoileoir leat agus an "miotal uilig ag lonrú leis faoin ghrian" i bhfad tar éis an dán a léamh.

Sa dán 'ÁÉÍÓÚ' le Liam Ó Muirthile cruthaítear laethanta bunscoile thiar sna seascaidí. Gnéith láidir den dán an bogadh atá ann idir an eagla agus an teacht slán, de réir mar a ghluaiseann an scála gutaí ó Á an scanraidh go an Ú "i dtiúin" i ndeireadh a dáin luascann sé idir an t-imeaglú agus an fhuascailt agus idir an gníomh brúidiúil agus an gníomh instinniúil. Ar scoil i rang an Bhráthar Dermo, caitear gnéithe aiceanta an domhain a mharcáil ar léarscáileanna agus tugtar "greadadh ó thalamh" don té go dteipeann air:

> …is an Bráthair ag rá
> idir buillí de liú:
> "Ní hea ansan ach ansan"
> á aistriú soir an chuid is lú.

Tráthnóntaí samhraidh, áfach, téitear:

> …ag snámh i Muir Chairbre
> ar Inse an Duine sna Bahámaí
> láimh le trópaicí Chloich na Coillte…

Ar scoil caitear fanacht ag seasamh "sa chlós/gan oiread is lámh ná cos a chorraí", ach lá amháin cuirtear abhaile ón scoil na buachaillí agus an Bráthair tíoránta seo, a deireadh "Tá milseán agam duit" ag tagairt dá bhata sara bpleancadh sé buachaill, ag rá leo anois:

> …guí le dúthracht
> go gcasfadh loingeas na Rúise
> go dtiocfadh ciall chuig Kruschev,
> is chonac cuntanós an Bhráthar
> á chomhleá ina dhuine buartha.

Sin an Bráthair ina dhuine agus i ndeireadh an dáin nuair a chíonn an buachaill atá ina fhear fásta anois an bráthair ar thaobh na sráide bíonn fonn air labhairt leis, "Mise Hurley rang scoláireachta '62" a rá agus ar an tslí sin slánú éigin a thabhairt i gcrích ach teipeann air:

...an tuin a aimsiú
chun na focail a chur in iúl
go ndéanfadh buíochas díobh
ar scála ÁÉÍÓÚ i dtiúin.

sa tslí nach réadaítear an tsintéis ar an dá thaobh den luascadh a bhraitear tríd an dán, rud ar láidrede an dán é.

Seoid is ea an dán 'An Cailín ar Glaodh Amach Uirthi' le Micheál Ó Ruairc. Fanann an radharc seo leat faoi mar a fhanann sé i gcuimhne an fhile fhéin. N'fheadar ab é comhréir an fhrása tosaigh, an clásal indíreach, i dtús an dáin a bheireann ar an léitheoir nó díreach a shimplí is atá an friotal, ach cuirtear an léitheoir isteach sa radharc láithreach amhail is go bhfaca an léitheoir féin é. Leanann na mionsonraí ansin, a haghaidh ar dhath na luaithe, an t-atlas fágtha ar oscailt, an peann luaidhe a d'fhág an cailín ina diaidh leagtha fiarthrasna an leathanaigh. An gnáthshaol stoptha, léarscáil na hEorpa reoite faoi mar a bheadh an saol go léir reoite, agus an Mhuir Dhubh faoi mar a bheadh uaigh ann ar an leathanach, poll dubh é ag screadaíl i gcuimhne an fhile. Tá an dán chomh simplí leis sin, chomh déanta, glan, iomlán leis sin. An mhóimint tugtha chun beatha ar phár. An saghas cuimhne glé atá againn go léir is dócha ar mhóimint chinniúnach éigin, pé acu ab é ár gcinniúint fhéin é nó cinniúint duine éigin eile. An saghas dáin a chuireann éad ort mar fhile leis an té a scríobh.

Anoir ó Neipeal a thagann an dán 'Do Prashant: Gúrú i gClúidíní' le Cathal Ó Searcaigh chugainn. Prashant an mac sa teaghlach a casadh ar léitheoirí an leabhair *Seal i Neipeal* le Cathal atá i gceist sa dán. Cur síos ar iontas an linbh leis an saol agus ar an tslí ina dtéann an leanbh i ngleic leis an saol sin tríd an úsáid a bhaineann sé as teanga atá sa dán:

"...Níl lá dá n-éiríonn nach bhfuil tú, a ghúrú na gclúidíní, ag múnlú d'urlabhra uaibhreach féin, ag briatharú na beatha de spalpacha reatha...."

An saol á ainmniú as an nua ag an leaid óg, ainmneacha nua aige do laethanta na seachtaine "Dé Sú Úll, Dé Kathmandú, Dé Búda-Buí, Dé Daidí-na-Gealaí".

Ar shlí, áfach, is dán é seo faoi iontas an fhile leis an mbuachaill óg:

> …baineann tú as ár gcleachtadh sinn le héirim cinn
> do chuid cainte agus tú ag cur d'fhírinne úraoibhinn
> féin ar chiall na coitiantachta….

a deir an file. Tá an domhan á léiriú nó á chruthú fiú as an nua ag an leanbh seo don bhfile. Is é iontas seo an fhile i láthair an linbh agus an gean cneasta macánta atá aige dó a thagann tríd sa dán seo agus a dhéanann dán éagsúil de.

In 'Imram thar m'eolas' déanann Gabriel Rosenstock fiosracht agus samhlaíocht buachalla óig a chruthú agus ina theannta sin léiríonn sé an tslí ina maireann cuimhní áirithe ar feadh na mblianta mar an chuimhne ar an mboladh, mar shampla, a luaitear leis an tincéir mná a tháinig chun an dorais, "Cumhráin uile/na hAraibe? Allas na gcapall/Cannaí stáin os cionn bhladhmsach thine." Is mian leis an mbuachaill an réal déirce atá aige le tabhairt don mbean a chur síos idir a dhá chíoch agus nuair nach ligeann sí dó é sin a dhéanamh plabann sé an doras san aghaidh uirthi. Ach tá an deorantacht a chráfaidh an buachaill óg ina dhiaidh sin braite cheana féin. "Las rud éigin ina súile" a deir sé agus pé ní é sin a las ina súile tá sé ag dó na geirbe riamh ó shin aige go dtí an lá inniu féin faoi mar atá an réal nár thug sé don dtincéir mná á dhó agus á loscadh. Is é an tóir ar an rud dofhála atá á chruthú sa dán seo. Rud atá dofhála b'fhéidir de bhrí nach dtuigtear i gceart cad é féin, gur ní é atá thar eolas an fhile, thar eolas an duine. Go mbíonn rud éigin ann i gcónaí go mbímid sa tóir air, go gcaithfidh a bheith. An t-athrá ar an líne "shamhlaíos an Éigipt mhéith nó an Phuinseaib léi" a thugann an sireadh síoraí seo amach.

Filí éagsúla an deichniúr filí atá anseo. Guth sainiúil ag gach duine acu. An ní atá comónta eatarthu a gcumas agus an cúram a ghlacann siad i mbun focal. I gcionn fiche bliain nó i gcionn deich mbliain fiú n'fheadar a mbeidh trácht ar aon cheann de na dánta seo ach is maith an fómhar é dar liom an deich ndán seo in aon bhliain amháin. Déarfar is dócha go bhféadfaí níos mó dánta as ar foilsíodh le bliain anuas a chur leo, is go bhféadfaí cur leis an líon dánta Gaeilge i gcomparáid leis an mBéarla b'fhéidir, ach dar liom nach raibh aon ní eile ann i mbliana a bhí ar aon chaighdeán leo sin a roghnaigh mé agus nuair a chuirtear san áireamh an méid dánta Béarla a fhoilsítear in Éirinn in aon bhliain ar leith ní dócha go bhféadfaí dul mórán níos airde ná deich ndán i mbliana ach go háirithe.

Táim fíorbhuíoch d'eagarthóirí na n-irisí, agus den mhuintir eile sna hirisí éagsúla, a chuir ábhar ar fáil dom nó a chabhraigh liom teacht ar ábhar, táim buíoch d'fhoireann Leabharlann Chathair Chorcaí agus d'fhoireann na Leabharlainne Náisiúnta as an gcabhair a thugadar go flaithiúil freisin agus de na foilsitheoirí a chuir saothar a n-údar ar fáil dom.

Le déanaí cailleadh beirt fhear gur mhórphearsana ab ea iad i saol nuafhilíocht na Gaeilge le tríocha bliain anuas agus níos mó, duine acu i bhfíorthosach na tréimhse a chlúdaítear sa díolaim seo agus an duine eile i ndeireadh na tréimhse. Buanchara dá chomhfhilí riamh ab ea Michael Davitt. I dteannta na "bhfilí óga" eile a bhí i gColáiste na hOllscoile, Corcaigh, i ndeireadh na seascaidí chuir sé ardán ar fáil d'fhilí na Gaeilge tríd an dtréimhseachán *Innti* a bunaíodh sa bhliain 1970. Chomh maith le fuinneamh úr a chur i bhfilíocht na Gaeilge leis an bhfriotal nua-aimseartha gur bhain sé leas as, do b'fhéidir a rá, leis, gur thug sé an greann isteach sa nuafhilíocht, an greann fial fóbartach sin aige. Ba chrann taca i gcónaí é chomh maith d'fhilí ab óige ná é, ba é ár ngile mear é, ár mbligeard sráide. A Mhichael, cad is féidir a rá ach go gcoinneoimid orainn ag coinneáil orainn. Foilsíodh *Dánta 1966-1998* i ndeireadh an bliana 2004 agus bhí dhá chnuasach eile aige nach bhfuil tiomsaithe ansin, *Fardoras* agus *Seimeing Soir*. Tá teacht ar leaganacha Béarla dá shaothar sa chnuasach dátheangach *Freacnairc Mhearcair/The Oomph of Quicksilver.*

File, drámadóir agus scoláire ab ea Seán Ó Tuama. Mar léachtóir agus criticeoir chuir sé léirthuiscint ar an bhfilíocht, agus ar an nuafhilíocht ach go háirithe, chun cinn i measc mac léinn agus léiritheoirí na Gaeilge i gcoitinne. Chomh maith leis na staidéir acadúlacha Ghaeilge aige mar *An Grá in Amhráin na nDaoine* agus *Filí Faoi Sceimhle* chuir Seán le tuiscint lucht an Bhéarla ar litríocht na Gaeilge chomh maith trí *An Duanaire: Poems of the Dispossessed* a chur amach i gcomhar le Thomas Kinsella agus *Repossessions — Selected Essays on the Irish Literary Heritage*, leagan Béarla dá aistí critice Gaeilge a chur amach. Sna hochtóidí luatha léirigh Seán arís an tsuim a bhí aige sa litríocht reatha agus i scríbhneoirí óga a spreagadh trí shraith ceardlann scríbhneoireachta a chur ar bun i gColáiste na hOllscoile, Corcaigh agus sraith eile a eagrú ina dhiaidh sin faoi choimirce Aonad an Léinn Sheachtraigh i gColáiste na hOllscoile, Gaillimh. I measc na ndaoine a d'fhreastail ar na ceardlanna sin bhí go leor scríbhneoirí, idir fhilí agus phrósadóirí, a bhain cáil amach ó shin. Mairfidh tionchar Sheáin trí shaothar na scríbhneoirí sin chomh maith lena shaothar féin. Is maith liom fhéin cuimhneamh ar Sheán mar a chonac é i lár an tsamhraidh tráth, é féin agus Beití, is iad ag imeacht uaim tríd an ró samh ar Bhéal Bán faoi mar a bheidís ag "leá d'aonghnó sa teas".

Colm Breathnach
Léim an Bhradáin
Deireadh Fómhair, 2006

Introduction

These forty poems in English, by Irish poets or poets living in Ireland, were published in books, magazines and newspapers over the twelve-month period between July 2005 and July 2006. About a third appeared in Ireland, the rest in the US and the UK. They come from little-known, hard-to-find publications, as well as from prestigious imprints such as the New Yorker and the TLS. If nothing else, this selection reflects the broad geographical reach of places where poems from Ireland can turn up nowadays. It also shows the esteem — surely disproportionate for a small damp teddy-bear-shaped island? — which Irish poetry has earned throughout the Anglophone world.

Also — and this may not be such a good thing — the selection shows a remarkable degree of cultural cohesion. These poems, though they are by no means uniform, clearly share a tradition. They may be written in New England or eastern Europe but they are meant to be understood in Cork and Galway, and vice versa. They assume familiarity with our history; with our bogs and weather; and that we've all read our Yeats. There is indeed an assumption that Ireland has established a demotic culture and therefore we can project confidently into the world. This gives these poems a directness, energy and agility drawn from the vigour of vernacular language — whereas in the past Irish poetry often suffered from stylistic eccentricity. It found a virtue in a distinctive Irishness (Austin Clarke) or a resolute non-Irishness (Brian Coffey), and in both cases poetry was practised as a rather highbrow art — whereas today's poets have a welcome sense of audience.

The danger with such confidence is complacency. I confess that in my reading I found a lot that was garrulous and predictable, and noted a pretty generous tolerance among editors to put up with it. So, in making my selection, I was undoubtedly drawn to poems that do their job without too much fuss or sweat. Fergus Allen's poem about the castrato, which opens the selection, can be read many times before its ironies fully unfold. Not everything has that exquisite compression. Leontia Flynn's 'Drive' takes us for quite a spin but it is driven by its rigorous form; Paul Perry, a poet new to me, goes on a more hair-raising verbal rampage in 'The Gate to Mulcahy's Farm' but never quite loses control; in 'The Hook of Hamate', Kelly Sullivan, another new voice, makes a list, but what an inventive deadly list it is. In Rita Ann Higgins' 'Grandchildren', we are made to laugh, shiver, and finally brought close to tears within the compass of a half-page. This is the kind of work-rate I like in poems.

Some of those included are young enough to be my children. Several others are poets I grew up under: literary 'godfathers' whose work formed my taste in the 1970s. So, in a sense, this book — though strictly a snapshot of one year's work — is also a reflection of Irish poetry over half a century, a period when (to state the obvious) the country changed. I leave to readers to decide to what extent these poems measure up to the scale and pace of those changes. But, for me, the book was worth the effort alone just to come across 'Superfresh' from Thomas Kinsella — who was on the Leaving Certificate curriculum by the time I left school. This encounter, literally both brief and touching, with a Russian immigrant in a supermarket renews one's belief in poems as the best means by which the strangeness of experience is registered.

I have limited myself to one poem from each poet. Given the hundreds now publishing, this seemed a necessary restriction — but one which I suspect, say, thirty years ago might not have been as rewarding. A smaller roster with more poems per person would have worked better then. Also, one would have been hard put to find many women. Although the balance in this selection is still numerically in favour of the men, I'd suggest it may be a closer call in terms of weight.

But I didn't worry much whether a poem was by a man or a woman, or by someone famous or one I hadn't heard of. And I didn't think about the type of poems I was choosing or what they were about. I acted more like someone who climbs a small hill every morning and builds a cairn with those stones that catch the eye along the way. I didn't work towards an overall shape, convinced that an assortment is interesting for its variety. The contrast between poems, the way they rub against each other, can bring out their characteristics, the uniqueness of shape and sound that makes them memorable.

In making my heap, I had good help from Patrick Cotter, John McAuliffe and Kathryn Maris, each of whom I thank for bringing to my notice poems I might have missed (but no blame to them for those I have no doubt over-looked). When I was done, I put the names in alphabetical order, and here are the poems — each one I think an admirable example of craft, with perhaps a bit of luck in its making; each at least some small surprise to the mind, and in some cases, I trust, potent enough to quicken the heart rate.

Maurice Riordan

FERGUS ALLEN

Alessandro Moreschi, Castrato

When he was ten they snipped his little balls off,
This being in everyone's interest, including God's.
Now, said Padre Matteo, his angelic voice
Will save us all. Alesso was not consulted.

Today I heard it, the boyish treble that survived
The iron maiden of the twentieth century,
Still sparkling like acqua minerale con gas.
'Ave Maria!', he thinly trilled, 'Ave Maria!'.

Gas Light and Coke (Dedalus)

EAVAN BOLAND

And Soul

My mother died one summer —
the wettest in the records of the state.
Crops rotted in the west.
Checked tablecloths dissolved in back gardens.
Empty deck chairs collected rain.
As I took my way to her
through traffic, through lilacs dripping blackly
behind houses
and on curbsides, to pay her
the last tribute of a daughter, I thought of something
I remembered
I heard once, that the body is, or is
said to be, almost all
water and, as I turned southward, that ours is
a city of it,
one in which
every single day the elements begin
a journey toward each other that will never,
given our weather,
fail —
        the ocean visible in the edges cut by it,
cloud colour reaching into air,
the Liffey storing one and summoning
the other, salt greeting the lack of it at the North Wall, and,
as if that weren't enough, all of it
ending up almost every evening

inside our speech –
coast canal ocean river stream and now
mother – and I drove on and although
the mind is unreliable in grief, at
the next cloudburst it almost seemed
they could be shades of each other,
the way the body is
of every one of them and we
were all moving now – fog into mist,
mist into sea spray, and both into the oily glaze
that lay on the railings of
the house she was dying in
as I went inside.

The New Yorker

COLETTE BRYCE

Self-portrait (In the Dark with Cigarette)

To sleep, perchance
to dream? No chance:
it's 4 a.m. and I'm wakeful
as an animal,
loath to admit that without your heat
my body has lost the ability to sleep.
On the window seat, I light a cigarette
from a slim flame, and monitor the street
like a stilled film, bathed in amber,
softened now in the wake of a downpour.

Beyond the daffodils
on Magdalen Green, there's one slow vehicle
pushing its beam along Riverside Drive,
a sign of life;
and two months on
from 'moving on'
your car, that you haven't yet picked up,
waits in a glitter of raindrops like bubble wrap.
Here, I could easily go off
on a riff

on how cars, like pets, look a little like their owners
but I won't 'go there'
as they say in America
on account of the fact it's a Nissan Micra...
And you don't need to know that
I've been driving it illegally at night
in the lamp-lit silence of this city,
you'd only worry,
or, worse, that Morrissey
is jammed in the tape deck now and for eternity,

no. It's fine: all gleaming hubcaps;
seats like an upright, silhouetted couple.
From the dashboard, the wink
of that small red light I think
is a built-in security system.
In a poem
it could represent a heartbeat or a pulse.
Or loneliness; its vigilance.
Or simply the lighthouse-regular spark
of someone, somewhere, smoking in the dark.

Poetry London

MAIRÉAD BYRNE

I Went to the Doctor

I went to the doctor. It had been so long since I'd seen a doctor I thought she was trying to interview me. When we first met, she said: *Married, Single, Widowed, Divorced?* I thought that was a bit personal. But I told her about my children, my husbands, my job, my furnace, my fall. About how I slept like a top. And Gold's Gym. And the sunken garden in the Pendleton House which is a house inside a museum. And my famous story of how I immigrated 11 years ago with $400 and a 7-year old child. We talked about poetry. Well, duh. But it was actually much broader than most poetry interviews, looser yet more intense. She asked me about drug use. Marijuana. Cocaine. That made me laugh. Everyone was so interested in me. It was marvelous. Even the nurse in Reception asked as she was passing: *Do you happen to know your height?* Boy did I! Then the Office Manager arranged all my appointments. I haven't had so much attention since the MLA or my first wedding. I'm going back.

Fascicle 2

MOYA CANNON

The Train

The railway embankment to our left
drives a green line through scree and grizzled heather.
A ghost track carries a ghost train
west from Letterkenny to Burtonport.
On one of the slatted wooden seats sits
a serious fourteen-year-old from Tyrone
with fine, straight, reddish hair.
The train huffs and clanks over our heads
across tall, cut-stone pylons
which flank the narrowest part of the road.

She is travelling to Irish college in Ranafast
in nineteen twenty-nine.
The narrow-gauge train steams along so slowly
that she can reach out
and pull leaves off the occasional, passing tree.
Her friend holds her hat out of the window
and swizzles and swizzles it around, absent-mindedly,
until it spins off and lands amid the scree.

My mother does not know that the railway line was built
by men who believed that the train was foreseen
in the prophecies of Colmcille
as a black pig snorting through the gap.
She cannot prophesy, so she does not know
that her father will be dead within three years,

29

or that she will meet her husband
and will spend her adult life
west of these rounded, granite hills
or that, in seventy-five years time,
one of her daughters will drive her
under this disappeared bridge
and out of Donegal
for the last time.
All she knows is that she is going to Ranafast
and that the train is travelling very slowly.

Poetry Ireland Review

HARRY CLIFTON

McCrystal's

All night, on the opposite shore,
The lights of McCrystal's glitter.
You could walk on water
To get there, and be drowned,
Or take the long way round,

Where a million instants
Shatter and die on the windscreen –
Late summer insects, flecks of rain
Melting into each other again –
And change is the only constant.

There, where sky and water meet
And none are strangers to themselves
Or the land beneath their feet,
McCrystal, quietly stacking shelves,
Open infinitely late

On the universe, picks you out
From the fixed and wandering stars
Of sailmakers' cottages, nightbound cars –
Forever approaching, the only man
Driven by supernatural doubt.

Everything mortal shies away.
The horse in foal, and the fox
Dead in your headlights, oozing blood,
Glittering back an evil eye,
You too, my friend, will have to die...

And the goddesses, the gods,
Of summer – girls, bare-midriffed,
Riding shotgun through the moonroofs,
Running the double gauntlet
Of boyfriends and the temperance squad

The forecourt of his filling station
Blazes like broad daylight.
Ask – have you travelled all this way
Past trees and people, gable ends
Turning back on a western sky,

To cash a cheque? Or shatter the veil
Of phenomena? His Holy Grail
Is sand and futures, factory-floors,
Grazing rights on an airfield
Overgrown since the last World War...

Everything everyone needs he stores,
As self-contained as a man-god
In the aftermath of creation.
Anything else, from the farther shore,
Is optical, an illusion.

Poetry Ireland Review

Michael Davitt

Déirc
do Mhoira

Níor leor na silíní fiáine chun ár sciúch a fhliuchadh tar éis uair an chloig
de shiúlóid i mbeirfean an mheán lae. Bhí braoinín uisce uainn go géar.

Seana-bhean de dhéine shéimh Pheig Sayers
fé chruitín údarásach a d'oscail doras ársa an tí feirme *Gasconne.*

An mbeadh *un verre d'eau* aici? Bheadh agus bucaod!
is d'iompaigh sí láithreach uainn i dtreo fhionnuaire chrón na cistine.

An mar seo a bhí le déircínteacht fadó? Gan aon éileamh mór a dhéanamh
ach a bheith i láthair in am an ghátair agus an chruinne ag athroinnt a coda?

Ar nós an tseana-fhráma rothair leis an leathroth búclálta
a bhronn m'athair ar an dtincéir mná mar aon le púnt siúicre,

is chuimhníos im gharsún gurb shin an fáth go mbíonn seana-fhrámaí
                                                        rothair ann
is gurbh shin an chiall go ndeintear rothaí a bhúcláil.

D'fhill bean an uisce gan mhoill le crúiscín lán na déirce agus dhá ghloine
á rá go mbeadh a thuilleadh is a thuilleadh ann dúinn dá mba ghá.

Agus fíon fuar an tobair bheannaithe ag beannú ár scornacha
sheas ár seana-bhean i mbéal an dorais —

33

a haoibh roicneach ag lonrú as an scáil
fé mar gu'b'í féin a bhí ag fáil na déirce ón mbeirt thincéir.

Irish Pages / Duillí Éireann

GERALD DAWE

Points West

For Kevin and Eve

When the street has gone all so quiet
except for the police car that whizzes up
and down at the same time every night —

when the timbers jolt and the radiators click-click
and the action of the clock gets ready to strike —
I stumble across a blustery waste ground,

a cliff face, a dozen streets of little
houses, under a full moon, blinded by
the light of a door that's been left open,

church bells clanging at six in the morning,
the first train haring off to points west,
and, from the garden that edges a misty lake,

wind chimes accompany my 'going before me',
to the terrace overlooking a splendid sea,
where the kids hunt in rock pools or dive

headlong into the uplit swimming pool,
the smoky hills behind and beyond us
nestle the rich and no-longer famous —

ex-colonials on retreat and contemplatives –
but in the bulky containers moving so slowly,
stowaways crouch for pockets of air.

I am off again, daydreaming of marauding
tree wasps with their ghastly undercarriages,
cicadas ringing their nightly changes,

the high-pitched whine of a mosquito,
my eyes peeled on dolphin-watch,
while they, like dancers, wait in the wings.

London Review of Books

JOHN F. DEANE

Towards a Conversion

There is a soft drowse on the bog today;
the slight bog-cotton scarcely stirs; for now
this could be what there is of the universe, the far-off
murmuring of the ocean, the rarest traffic passing, barely

audible beyond the hill. I am all attention, held
like a butterfly in sunlight. I am in love
with this island earth, the fibrous, incandescent
unsouled ground, its necessary distance, its

familiarity. I can achieve, a while,
an orchid quiet, the tiny shivering of petals, the mere
energy of being. Along the cuttings
slow bubbles lift through black water

and escape, softly, into sunlight;
I have loved, always, the tough
up-bearing heather-springs and yielding moss;
this complex knotting of roots has been

an origin, and nothing new nor startling
will happen here, save the growth of sphagnum
into peat; if this is prayer, then
I have prayed. I walk over millennia, the Irish

wolf and bear, the elk and other
miracles; everywhere bog-oak roots
and ling, forever in their gentle
torsion, with all this floor a living thing, held

in the world's care, indifferent. Over everything
the predatory crow, a monkish body hooded
in grey, crawks its blacksod, cleansing music;
lay your flesh down here you will become

carrion-compost, sustenance for the ravening roots;
you will be, your self, a prayer, you will be
praise, present without guile, or art, or favour;
for something huge and undefeated looms,

something like truth, integrity, like dread. This, I think
is where my God is, this His home;
after the Iliads, the Odysseys, to return and lay
your head down on the familiar: God

is, is here, and will be. Sometimes a kestrel
appears from the shadow of the hill, and hovers —
all life beneath continuing, out of respect;
later you may come across some split feathers,

you may hear a terrified small squeal
of pain or fright; if you step too fast a snipe
will explode out of the cuttings to startle
the very air about it; listen for the harmonies

a lingering sadness makes in a counterpoint
to peace. And be converted: to the bleak
bones of necessity, to the languorous
leaching of life's fluids, to the slow,

the concentrated obedience of peat
and root and scutch to their Creator.
Turn then, and move back quietly to the road,
your footprints on the soft earth already fading.

PN Review

GREG DELANTY

Aceldama

And Judas cast down the pieces of silver in the temple, and departed. And the priests and elders took counsel, and bought with the pieces of silver the potter's field, to bury strangers in. Wherefore that field has been called, The Field of Blood, unto this day.

Matthew 27:5-8

We drove down what seemed the curve
of the earth, sandwiched in our Ford Anglia.
We were happy as the colours of our beachball,
a careless car full of mirth and singalong songs,
songs that were mostly as sappy
as the soppy tomato sandwiches sprinkled with sand,
which is why they're called sandwiches our father said,
sandwiched himself now in the ground between his mother
and ours. What's the meaning of dead?
Which one of us children asked that as we passed
the spot with the lit steel cross on Carr's Hill,
putting the kibosh on the next song,
our mother about to break into *Beautiful City?*
She crossed herself, saying that's the place they bury
those whose lives somehow went wrong, betrayed
in one way or other, without a song to their names,
or a name, everyone buried together
and alone without a headstone.
The crepuscular loneliness of the field
shrouded our bright time. Our world,
the city below, shimmered like the silver pieces
scattered on the dark floor of the temple.

Collected Poems 1986 - 2006 (Carcanet)

KATIE DONOVAN

Buying a Body

I would go to the mall
in my white rental car,
and shop for a new heart for you,
father; choose lungs,
as strong and light
as parachutes.
I would purchase
the finest pair of wrists,
the fastest feet,
and legs as fleet
as a stag's.
I would go
to the sleep dispenser
and find you dreams
blue and serene
as your favourite summer sky.
I'd buy you time.
But I'm home
from the land of malls,
and I've turned in
the rental car.
It's just you and me
in the cold Sunday afternoon,
you gasping as the lamb
you thought your hands could hold
slips free; the mother bleating,
me not moving as quick
as you'd like
to shut the gate.

You urge me up the yard
the lamb's black legs
in my fist, and I wonder
why it takes so long for you
to follow.
I learn later
you're hardly able to walk it now,
but today you aimed
to pull the wool
over my eyes.

The Irish Times

TOM DUDDY

Side Street

I don't often pass through this part of the city,
though it's on my way uptown as the crow flies.
I don't feel at home here, or streetwise — it's cold,
even when the sun is warming the chimneys,

and dark to boot. My footsteps lose their beat,
the paths are so skewed, so irregular here.
The people are not the same as mainstreet people —
a woman comes dashing out of the shoe repair

(Heels-While-U-Wait) shop and cries sorry; pieces
of burnt paper float from somewhere behind me,
and the man loping rapidly ahead of me
without looking back shouts 'Shag off, will ye!'

(but not angrily) at some guys just out of range
of the corner of my eye. They say nothing at all,
these guys, as the loper increases his lead,
nor do they overtake me. The hot sharp smell

of burnt paper darts to the back of my throat,
and I think a small fragment, like a green flake
of distemper from the wall of an old porch,
has landed on my shoulder, but I can't check

or be seen to brush it off. Stepping into mainstreet
is like returning through the looking-glass without
a moment's notice — shoppers tucked in behind me,
not a thing on my shoulder, slight catch in my throat.

Magma 33

PAUL DURCAN

Let the Hierarchy Go Play Croquet in Honolulu

I was playing for the Over 50s
In a football game against the Under 50s
In the park on the quays
When the referee broke the news
That the priest with two children had told the archbishop
To take a running jump for himself,
Bernadette's sweet, decent priest with the fork-lift smile.
We continued the game and in the dying seconds
I scored the winner with a header,
A spurting, ecstatic header
No crimson hierarch
Would have divined, much less celebrated
The art and the mystery of,
Not even a primate of the hierarchy
Taking a running jump for himself.
As my head made contact with the ball,
I knew I was doing it for the priest with two children,
That sweet, decent man with the fork-lift smile.
If only Bernadette had been alive to see my goal
But she had died of a heart attack
Watching the pope's funeral on television.
Let the hierarchy go play croquet in Honolulu:
Grass-skirts, mallets, hoops, balls;
The whole jing-bang hula-hoopla.

The Irish Times

LEONTIA FLYNN

Drive

My mother's car is parked in the gravel drive
outside the house. A breeze springs
from the shore, and blows against this traffic sign,
standing between the byroad and the main road,
where somewhere a cricket ticks like a furious clock.
My mother's car is an estimable motor,

a boxy thing – the car in which my mother,
during a morning's work will sometimes drive
to Dundrum, Ballykinlar, Seaford, Clough,
"Newcastle", "Castlewellan", "Hiltown", "Analong".
They drive along the old roads and the new roads –
my father, in beside her, reads the signs

as they escape him – for now they are empty signs,
now one name means as little as another;
the roads they drive along are crumbling roads.
- "Dromore", "Banbridge" (my father's going to drive
my mother to distraction) "In Banbridge town…", he sings.
She turns the car round, glancing at the clock

and thinks for a moment, turning back the clock,
of early marriage – love! – under the sign
of youth and youthful fortunes – back, in the spring,
the first *great mystery* of life together:
my mother's indefatigable drive
keeping them both on the straight and narrow road;

and, as they pass "Killough" or "Drumaroad",
she thinks of children – broods a while (cluck cluck),
on their beginnings (this last leg of this drive
leads back to the empty house which she takes as a sign)
and how does it work, she thinks, this little motor?
Where are its cogs, and parts and curly oiled springs

that make her now, improbably, the wellspring
of five full persons – out upon life's highroads:
a grown up son, a gang of grown up daughters,
prodigal, profligate – with 30 years on the clock?,
she doesn't know, and isn't one to assign
meaning to their ways, their worlds' bewildering drives –

though she tells offspring she's nearing the end of the road
a clock ticks softly … the low pulse of some *drive*…?
My mother watches. She's waiting for a sign…

Poetry London

ANNE-MARIE FYFE

Curaçao Dusk

A plane flies off a map's edge
today. At the console O'Hara inhales
the ozone of Curaçao Dusk.
Manilla postcards, weightless with
preprinted greetings, flutter in confined
space, franked, illegibly signed.
The manifest's well under payload.
Faces in cabin windows are graven
waxy masks, their sightlines
uninterrupted by pitchy flights
of eastbound ebony swans.
The hold's a chaos of tethered
cockatiels, small gods from Surinam.
Bursting valises disgorge wrist-watches,
standby parachutes, a crushed trumpeter's
mute. The co-pilot stows
isobar charts, taps the compass
twice for luck: he mouths a childhood
formula under clearwater skies
before resuming routine announcements
to the remnants of a cabin crew.

The Ghost Twin (Peterloo)

48

PEGGIE GALLAGHER

Letter to my Children

When I'm dead put me in a box with a fat book,
thermos, good dark chocolate, a *loc* of sonnets;
ones with a stake through the heart. The photographs
I never got to sort. A torch. Don't forget the torch.

The satin lining with a whiff of lily, ruched
and slippery. Portents of menace and mercy…
Rumours of resin, mortise and tenon *sans* rivets
or lead. Worms overhead. Earth settling on the lid.

Forget all that grave-tending lark. The dead don't give
a rap. The soul is not in residence. It's out there
somewhere desperately seeking *Flight Exit*.
(I never was one for finding my way easy.)

Watch sometime, when a shadow tracks the evening grass,
or, perhaps, when a small bird crashes the glass.

Southword

SAM GARDINER

Sorrow's Other Madness

Dawn, wearing golden sandals,
had broken into the bedroom
while he slept and was toying
with the lids of his eyes.

He woke early and lay late
in one of her dreams,
happy to pretend again,
before staggering brokenly out

into a sultry July morning.
Unfed and unshaved, he drilled
a ton of forage rape straight into
the winter barley stubble.

Poetry London

EAMON GRENNAN

The Search

It's the sheer tenacity of the clematis clinging to
rusted wire and chipped wood-fence that puts this
sky-blue flare and purple fire in its petals. To be
new in autumn, in mid-September, to be showing
yourself like that, naked as water under full moonlight:

something has to be good in such a world, in the
talent it has for lasting and coming back, in the way
it decorates our graves, our standing walls, our back
porches, and in the way the late bee lands on its
dazzle, walks the circumference of every petal

in some minor key of astonishment — drinking
the last of its sapphire wine. What takes shape
is a cellular sense of how the moment is jammed
to splitting with excess, each pod and sweet kernel
plumped to bursting with the brash simplicities

of contradiction, the child's tears watering the plant
that seems from a shrivel of bones to make itself
an azure conflagration, seeming to say There's
always more to say. Language can be like that,
taking its stand on the driest, most barren space

of clay, asking only that we attend, behold it being
no more than being itself — a nothing, blooming.
And tonight the old man, your father, smiled twice:
once when he'd reached the sofa after the fifty-mile
shuffle from the hall door; once when his tongue

tasted the tart cool of a spoonful of blueberries and he
turned his eyes, shining their milky blue, on the child
who lifted her brimming spoon and smiled back at him.

The Threepenny Review

VONA GROARKE

The Game of Tennis in Irish History

Blame Lady Alice Howard and her diary of 1873
patrolling the white line around the one green space
at Shelton Abbey where the Parnells, Charlie and Fanny,

banter back and forth, skirting the net, filling the hours
between politics and tea. She looks up: a weak breeze riffles
the pages on which she has pinned down the afternoon

in Indian ink, and their laughter scatters in choked aspen trees
where sunlight, regardless, upends both the game
and the ambitions of those plainly put-down words.

Another volume: Spring 1921. The diary laments
they have had a blow: a permit for the motor was refused.
Not so in Ballyturin House, where the tennis party

has broken up in salvered tea and calls for a reprise.
Which might itself have been an entry from the diary,
save for the culminating flourish of bodies, one slumped

over the fender like an umpire checking the chalk for dust
or the volley of shots like a flurry of late calls, or the opening
account of play stalled on the lodge gates oddly closed.

After that, it's a holding game, put down to delivery,
service skills, to foot faults or to where advantage falls
and to how often the metaphor is required to work the line

between incident and outrage, between the ins and outs
of the intent or outcome, to the calling out or not in
or only just, to the over and eventual out, out, out.

Poetry Wales

KERRY HARDIE

Countrymen
for Jim Barco

We were sitting in the Abbey waiting,
and he was telling me, low-voiced,
about their week-old spaniel pups,
the one with the tail that was two-thirds brown,
white only near the tip.

If he did it right, he said,
if he cut for the flash,
she'd be like the mother, her tail over-long,
always bloody after hunting,
ribboned
by furze and briar –
Ah, to hell with the theory,
the theory and the purists.
Blaze or no blaze, he'd cut her short.
He'd not see her hurt like Jess.

It was November,
the old year was slipping, the new one
drawing closer.
There were monks drifting through,
you could feel them – uncertain,
pressed close to the walls and in the worn places –
summoned to mark these eight hundred years
of the Abbey's grey stones in the valley.

He would do it himself?
He would, he said. A hot knife – fast – the heat sealing
the cut flesh. His hands mimed
the knife and the pup, I watched them.
the swift, sure cut,
against the dark wood, the monks drawing in
for a better look. I thought of our pups –
warm flesh-sacks, they'd jumped in my hands
as the clippers closed, and of the small bloody heap
on the vet's table. The monks were remembering
the oddness of hands, smells, blood, you could feel them
growing focused, denser, remembering
the body's red roar
    and the past stretching back
till it slid off the edge of time and the world,
and always a dog and a man –
through first light, through last light –
a man and a dog moving always together.

New Hibernia Review

SEAMUS HEANEY

The Blackbird of Glanmore

On the grass when I arrive,
Filling the stillness with life,
But ready to scare off
At the very first wrong move.
In the ivy when I leave.

It's you, blackbird, I love.

I park, pause, take heed.
Breathe. Just breathe and sit
And lines I once translated
Come back: 'I want away
To the house of death, to my father

Under the low clay roof.'

And I think of one gone to him,
A little stillness dancer –
Haunter-son, lost brother –
Cavorting through the yard,
So glad to see me home,

My homesick first term over.

And think of a neighbour's words
Long after the accident:
'Yon bird on the shed roof,
Up on the ridge for weeks –
I said nothing at the time

But I never liked yon bird.'

The automatic lock
Clunks shut, the blackbird's panic
Is shortlived, for a second
I've a bird's eye view of myself,
A shadow on raked gravel

In front of my house of life.

Hedge-hop, I am absolute
For you, your ready talkback,
Your each stand-offish comeback,
Your picky, nervy goldbeak –
On the grass when I arrive,

In the ivy when I leave.

District and Circle (Faber)

RITA ANN HIGGINS

Grandchildren

It's not just feasible at the moment
one daughter tells me.
What with Seamus still robbing banks
and ramming garda vans when he gets emotional
on a fish-free Friday in February.

Maybe the other daughter could deliver.
She thinks not, not at the moment anyway
while Thomas still has a few tattoos to get,
to cover any remaining signs that might link him
with the rest of us.

Just now a B52 bomber flies over
on its way from Shannon
to make a gulf in some nation's genealogy.

The shadow it places on all our notions is crystal clear
and for a split of a second helping
it juxtaposes the pecking order.
Now bank robbers and tattooers
have as much or as little standing
as popes and princes
and grandchildren become another lonely utterance
impossible to pronounce.

Throw in the Vowels: Selected Poems (Bloodaxe)

BIDDY JENKINSON

Guthanna Sinseartha

Fál sceach á chur agam
Lá Fhéile Bríde, lá bog tais,
ceobhrán allasach báistí anuas.
Pé áit a aimsíonn béal na láí
cúil chré sa chlochrach
déanaim poll, sáim fréamh,
cuirim spalla anuas uirthi.

Táim teanntaithe ag mo chóta.
Bainim é
agus cloisim mo mhamó agus mo shean-aintín
ag fógairt d'aon ghuth
'Cast not a clout till May is out.'
Caithim uaim mo hata.

Ní aimsím cré ar an gcéad amas eile
nó ar an dara ceann.
Leanann an láí ag bualadh creige.
Lúbann an líne curadóireachta
agus cloisim curfá na scál:
'Níl an líne sin díreach!'
'Cast not a clout. . .!'

Fáisceann thart orm an veist gheimhridh
a chuirtí orm, im leanbh, ag tús na Samhna
mar d'ordaigh Dia, cosaint ar an eitinn
– cniotáilte de bháinín oíliúil garbh –

le cneas,
go deireadh Bhealtaine...
'...till May is out!'

'Seafóid,' a deirim leis na taibhsí,
atá suite i dtom aitinn, ag cnáimhseáil.
(Is maith liom taibhsí.
Deimhníonn siad , ar shlí,
go mbeidh mé féin anseo timpeall,
ar ball.)
'Ní mí na Bealtaine a bhí i gceist in aon chor
ag bhur sinsir ónar fhoghlaim sibhse an nath.'
– Plandóirí ón mBreatain Bheag ab ea iad –
'An May a bhí i gceist acu ná bláth
na sceiche gile.
Iomrall teanga a choinníodh an veist sin orm
gach aon bhliain, 'till May is out.

Sceitheann sceacha geala i lár mhí Bealtaine.
B'shin coicís den tochas,
de bhreis ar a raibh dlite acu siúd,
a leag sibh orm,'
a deirim leo agus mé ag damhsa ar an bplanda nua-churtha
lena dhaingniú.

'Lena chois sin, tháinig bhur sinsir i bhfus
sular leasaigh an Pápa Gréagóir an féilire.
Bhíodh bláth bán ar an sceach
ag tús na Bealtaine nuair a cumadh an nath.
B'shin mí iomlán den léine róin sa bhreis
ar a raibh ceaptha.

'Agus lena chois sin fós, bhíodh na Breatnaigh
ag tagairt do *Crateagus Oxyacanthoides*
a d'fhásadh ar imeall coille, a bhláthaíodh
coicís roimh *Crateagus Monagyna*
nár leath ar fud na hÉireann go dtísna h*Enclosures*.

B'shin sé seachtainí péine a d'fhulaingíos
in aghaidh na bliana
de bharr míthuiscintí teanga is staire is bitheolaíochta.
Céard déarfas sibh anois?

Aimsíonn mo láí poll méith
mar ar ramhraigh raithneach agus aiteann an chré.
'Cast not a clout till May is out!'
Fógraíonn siad orm d'aon ghuth ó bharr chrann spíne.

Labhraíonn taibhsí
ach ní éisteann siad linn.

Oíche Bhealtaine (Coiscéim)

Thomas Kinsella

Superfresh

I pulled my trolley to one side
into the recess with the special bread
to find the list in one of my pockets
and check the next choices.
The leather overcoat wet and heavy,
the high collar still raw against my beard
from the snow.

    A woman stopped
in front of me. Her face thin,
her voice sharp.
     In what
have I offended...?

       But she was asking,
in a thick accent, where I came from; saying
that she came from Russia.
She stood there, no longer young,
waiting for an answer.

I understood; and told her
where I came from. Her eyes faded.
She spoke again, her voice distant, saying
something nondescript and lonely.
Our spirits disengaged, somewhere
above the Alps.

In my leather overcoat; in from the Winter;
bearded; not from Russia;
I touched the backs of my fingers

against her cheek, abstract-intimate,
in a fragrance off the shelves
of Italian loaves and French boule.

PN Review

NICK LAIRD

Initial Appraisal

Features? Embarrassed of their faeces,
omnivorous and sad, awkward beasts
dependent on their tightly metred breath

to keep on feeding, sleeping, breeding.
Oddly they prohibit eating certain species,
like guinea pigs or golden lemurs,

any kind of creatures who can crease
their hairless faces into wrinkles: amusement,
is it, or the purest, dumbest recognition.

They laugh, yes and snort, and stifle sneezes,
and though they sport the same thin fleeces
in the southern droughts and northern freezes,

so instinctively aggressive is the genus
that they herd in such a way to leave the weakest
prey to what might find it easiest to eat.

Still, wide-eyed in the darkness they fear it.
Part-rational, part-mammal, poor bastards,
forever yanked along on leashes by their genes.

Their minds may shine with language, yes,
but what good's that? Words are just pieces, like they are,
poor fuckers, who sit by themselves in the small hours,

warming a grievance, talking aloud, articulating
tiny myths of struggle and deliverance.
I did find something in them almost pleasing.

The Stinging Fly

MICHAEL LONGLEY

Proofs

I have locked overnight in my antique Peugeot
At the channel, close to stepping stones, the proofs
Uncorrected, of my forty years of poetry. What
Would I add to the inventory? A razor shell,
A mermaid's purse, some relic of this windless
Sea-roar-surrounded February quietude?

The Irish Times

JOHN MCAULIFFE

A Pyramid Scheme

An old Cortina's come to rest
At the end of the road. The weeks pelt
Its glass and steel, invisibly
Emptying it and making free

With the usual visitor, some random person,
Who strips the interior, then
Accompanied, helps himself
To tyres, axle, driveshaft, exhaust.

The bodywork flakes and scabs.
Going nowhere, looking naked, mad,
Mirrorless and windowless,
It gathers accessories

Like one of those disused roadside crannies:
Plastic bags, a seatful of empties
And, adjacent, a holed mattress, a pallet,
A small fridge – the whole lot useless, inside out,

Till the rusting shell starts half-stories
The kind that make it first notorious
For the children who will have to learn
What goes on at night, or could go on,

Then a shelter for their elders,
A try-out zone, its vacant doorless
Frame a guarded hiding-place, its fag-end
Still paying a dividend.

Poetry Ireland Review

THOMAS MCCARTHY

Moonlight Cooler, 1948

It was the four frosted tiki-stem cocktail glasses,
Survivors of a disreputable Irish bar in Minneapolis,
That you were most proud of on the day
Of the Ballysaggart races; that day when a man
Claiming to be Bing Crosby, or Bing's brother.
Walked into the pub with a Fine Gael Senator.
Both wore dinner jackets. The Senator's hunter
Had been lamed, hence the intense celebration
To mask his personal sadness. Two women,
Elegant and loud, followed them indoors:
Mrs Norah Foley said they were like goddesses,
The way they could move without moving, so to speak —
She watched them with the eyes of a wet
Sheep-dog as she threw lumps of turf on the fire.
You were non-plussed when they mentioned
The word 'cocktail', thinking to embarrass us all
In the parishes of Ballysaggart and Lismore.
Sure every baptised Christian in the county knew,
In them days, that on a moonlit evening in November
Two ladies on the way to dinner at a Big House
Would have the juice of one lemon, a little sugar,
Two Irish ounces of Calvados, and soda; all
Shaken with a bit of ice from O'Connor's fish store
And strained into — pardon the lack of highballs —
Your tiki-stem cocktail, glasses fit for any Bing.

The Irish Times

PETER MCDONALD

44A

I was trying to recall, and find words for,
the heavy sigh of our front door

pulling shut on its air-spring,
the small, mosquito-high ringing

of a timer-light out in the hall,
and the ox-blood colour of the tiles;

all from my narrow perch abroad
at the very hour you died.

*

In the optician's chair that day
beads of light were sore and dry

as I watched for a puff of air
that would reveal the blood-pressure

inside each open, waiting eye:
the thing is not to flinch, to try

to keep a steady head; I flinched;
we tried again; again I flinched.

*

A winter's day in Woodview Drive,
much like the days when you drove

home through twilight in a Ford
Prefect, and the sunset flared

between its windscreen and the rain;
or the rusty Mini, the sky-blue Austin

eleven-hundred, cars you tended
after their best days had ended,

*

The crazy paving, a foot wide,
never cemented, wobbled outside

our front window, where I found
my balance on one stone, and stood

poised, back to the roughcast wall,
like the boy-king of the Braniel,

with toes, feet, ankles and knees
shifting my own weight in the breeze.

*

It would take the light from your eyes —
I know; and it's hardly a surprise,

it's hardly news: that I should find
cold air at the gable-end

strange, or your face then, full
of the fear of death, terrible;

outside is empty, and goes away
fast as light this winter day.

                    *

Dead pieces in my life begin
to join up, one by one,

and now the Braniel falls below
my feet; the houses start to go,

as I keep steady in a place
made out of distances and space,

a prodigy of balance, where
the last breath is a breath of air.

TLS

73

DEREK MAHON

Jardin du Luxembourg
(after Rilke)

A merry-go-round of freshly painted horses
sprung from a childish world vividly bright
before dispersing in adult oblivion
and losing its quaint legendary light
spins in the shadows of a burbling circus.
Some draw toy coaches but remain upright;
a roebuck flashes past, a fierce red lion
and every time an elephant ivory-white.

As if down in the forest of Fountainebleau
a little girl wrapped up in royal blue
rides round on a unicorn; a valiant son
hangs on to the lion with a frantic laugh,
hot fists gripping the handles for dear life;
then that white elephant with ivory tusks —
an intense scrum of scarves and rumpled socks
though the great whirligig is just for fun.

The ring revolves until the time runs out,
squealing excitedly to the final shout
as pop-eyed children gasp there in their grey
jackets and skirts, wild bobble and beret.
Now you can study faces, different types,
the tiny features starting to take shape
with proud, heroic grins for the grown-ups,
shining and blind as if from a mad scrape.

TLS

DOROTHY MOLLOY

Life Boat

I made an ark out of my skull, an upturned hull with no mast, sail
or rigging,
except the switch of hair that still grew wild, as when I was
a child,
around the everlasting fontanelle.

I blocked the holes, I brushed the curving bone with bitumen
and pitch.
Safe from the world, I hid there all alone, till suddenly
dark stirrings
of my mind released the beasts within:

the onocentaur, oversexed, came rushing in; the manticora
grinding
all its teeth; the bonnacon with flaming bum; the fierce
monocerous;
the crocodile, the savage spotted pard;

the great baboon; the parandrus, the asp, the flying jaculus,
the seps.
At loggerheads, we drifted towards Armenia atop
the rising flood
and teetered on the pinnacles of Ararat.

For forty days or weeks or months or years, I waited
for the waters
to subside. The creatures in my cranium increased
and multiplied.
I said my prayers. I cried. The might of heaven

pounded on my roof. At last, the muddy hydrus
(the only serpent
on the side of the angels) led me out. And lo, God's gifts
lay scattered
all about: rare Paracletes with tongues of fire;

an Englishman with ropes and gamp; a singing bird, an olive branch,
a box of nard,
a spirit-lamp, safe passage to the cedar-groves of Lebanon.

Gethsemane Day (Faber)

PATRICK MORAN

Scruples

Imagine fretting that a play you wrote
sent out some men the English shot.

Or me wondering if any words of mine
could make these knowing countrymen

even pause in dispensing fungicides,
or spare one hedgerow from their blades.

Southword

PAUL MULDOON

At Least They Weren't Speaking French

I
At least they weren't speaking French
when my father sat with his brothers and sisters, two of each, on
   a ramshackle bench
at the end of a lane marked by two white stones
and made mouth music as they waited chilled to the bone

fol-de-rol fol-de-rol fol-de-rol-di-do

for the bus meant to bring their parents back from town.
It came and went. Nothing. One sister was weighed down
by the youngest child. A grocery bag from a town more distant still,
   in troth.
What started as a cough

fol-de-rol fol-de-rol fol-de-rol-di-do

would briefly push him forward to some minor renown,
then shove him back, oddly summery, down
along the trench
to that far-flung realm where, at least, they weren't speaking French.

II

At least they weren't speaking French
when another brother, twenty-something, stepped on a nail no one
    had bothered to clench
in a plank thrown
halfheartedly from the known to the unknown

fol-de-rol fol-de-rol fol-de-rol-di-do

across a drainage ditch on a building site. His nut brown arm. His
    leg nut-brown.
That nail sheathed in a fine down
would take no more than a week or ten days to burgeon from the froth
of that piddling little runoff

fol-de-rol fol-de-rol fol-de-rol-di-do

and make of him a green and burning tree. His septicemia-crown.
Sowens as much as he could manage. Trying to keep that
    flummery down
as much as any of them could manage. However they might
    describe the stench,
as exhalation, as odour, at least they weren't speaking French.

III

At least they weren't speaking French
when those twenty-something council workers, one with a winch,
   the other a wrench,
would point my son and me to the long overgrown
lane marked by two faded stones

fol-de-rol fol-de-rol fol-de-rol-di-do

like two white-faced clowns
gaping at the generations who passed between them and set down
bag after grocery bag. Setting them on the table. The newspaper
   tablecloth
1976. Not the East Tyrone Brigade, Not Baader-Meinhof

fol-de-rol fol-de-rol fol-de-rol-di-do

bringing the suggestion of a frown
to those two mummer-stones still trying to lie low, trying to keep
   their mummery down
to a bare minimum, two stones that, were they to speak, might blench
as much at their own giving out as our taking in that at least they
   weren't speaking French.

The New Yorker

GERRY MURPHY

Visitation
(after Apollonius Rhodius)

It was during that sea-grey hour
when darkness seems ready to yield the horizon
to the push of impending day.
We reached the deserted island of Thynias
and clambered down exhausted
onto the welcoming shore,
our hearts at last beginning to lighten.
As if on cue, Apollo, on his way
from Lycia to the slumbering haunts
of those innumerable Hyperboreans,
appeared over our heads.
In his left hand his silver bow,
on his shoulder a full quiver of arrows,
his golden hair framing
his immortal face.
Those of us who saw him
felt a sudden, uncontrollable dismay
and burst into tears.
The whole island trembled
beneath our feet as he passed
and the sea swelled alarmingly
and crashed onto the beach.
None of us dared to look at him directly,
we stood stock still, heads bowed,
until he vanished into the brightening distance.

The Irish Times

Fuascailt

Ba ghile, doimhne aon smior smear amháin seo
Ná fiche bliain tochailte craicinn le haon fhear;
I mbinneas na siosarnaí áille
I bhfáilteachas gach cnámh ar chnámh
I bhfuascailt anama a chuid ceoil cholainne.

Míle bliain a tháinig sé chuici
Seanachorp ársa, óg is oscailte in aon turas
Meon aigne níos doimhne ná uiscí na farraige
Geasa a ghlélúidín ar a gnúis
A mheall siar í go tús ama.

Anam le hanam ar feadh scaithimh.
Gan glór le cloisint ach fuaim dhraíochta
Gan aon fhocal pras ná íseal
Ach paidrín fada corónach chun na bhflaitheas.

Tugadh ar thuras an oíche sin í
A chealaigh aon chos ar chos a chuaigh roimis
Corp a sáthadh go smior, gan peaca uirthi ach a hóige
Pian a srac ina dhá leath í le mire
Gníomh a sháigh idir a dhá súil í le náire
Is eagla níos corraithe ná lá stoirme
A d'fháisc sí ina haigne feadh a saoil.

Do tháinig a saighdiúir maitheasa
Is scaoil sé geasa an oilc
D'oscail sé bláth a maighdeanais thréigthe
Is do chan sé léithe go ciúin.
Mar a bheadh radharc bharra cnoic lá gréine
Do leath an ghrian ar a cosa
Do chuala sí cantan na manach
Leath sí a sciatháin mhóra ar mhaitheas an tsaoil
Leagadh lámh ar leochaileacht a hanama
Is tháinig sí aghaidh ar aghaidh léithe féin den gcéad uair.

Seacht maslaí agus maisle ort, a fhir,
A shantaigh cuid colainne do chomharsan
Báite i nduibhe dhorcha ar feadh tríocha bliain
Gur leagadh solas ar uafás an ghnímh.

Do sheas sí faoi sholas na gealaí
Ach ní raibh aon gha ann;
Do sheas sí faoi bháthadh na gréine
Ach níor bhraith sí aon teas;
Do bháigh sí í féin in uiscí gorma
Ach ní raibh aon fhliuchras ann;
Tar chúichi arís, a thaibhse fir,
Go leagfaidh sí a géaga ar do chorp
Go bpógfaidh sí do dhá shúil
Go luífidh sí siar chun suain.

Mar ná fuil ar an saol seo
Ach lasair a bhíonn faoi dhoircheacht
Is do scaoil mo shaighdiúirín an gheas.
Feictear anois mé
Faoi sholas na gealaí.
Dóitear anois mé
Faoi theas na gréine.
Is téim ag snámh in uiscí gorma

Go n-ólaim fliuchras an tsáile
Im steillbheathaidh.

An Trodaí agus dánta eile / The Warrior and other poems (Cló Iar-Chonnachta)

Nuala Ní Dhomhnaill

Muisiriúin

Ba mhaith liom a bheith im' mhuisiriún,
óm bhaithis síos go dtí bundún
im chlár nimhe, ag fógairt oilc,
ag bagairt báis ar shlua an tsuilt.

Do bheinn chomh dúr le taobh an chlaí,
fuarspreosach, modartha, díomhaoin,
púiciúnta, iomlán faoi neamhshuim
ar bhuartha daoine, is ar a maoin.

Bheadh craiceann tais orm sleamhain, slim
é cruaidh is bog san am chéanna.
D'fhásfainn ar bhualtrach bó is ar chrainn
ag sú na maitheasa astu go ciúin.

D'fhásfainn san oíche i gan fhios
don saol maith mór, is do lucht an eolais.
Do bheinn níos lú ná tor nó craobh
ach phéacfainn suas thar phaiste sméar.

D'fhásfainn gan mhairg ar gach a d'éag.
Do shúfainn tríothu go dtín bpréamh,
go sroisfinn síos go dtí créafóig
is stopfainn ann is thabharfainn póg

don mbás, don bhfuarbholadh ceobhráin,
don meath, don néal, don bhfeochadán,
don dtaisríocht fuar is don bhfliuchán
don drúcht millteach, don sú sileáin.

Nár lige Dia go mbainfir greim
as an nathair bhreac, nó an púca peill,
an balbhán béice, an chaidhp bháis.
Níl insint scéil ar an bpianpháis

a leanann iad, an céasadh ceart.
Níl leigheas le fáil ná aon teacht as.
Is bheinn go sásta ina measc
ag ídiú saoil, ag scaipeadh báis.

Bheinn obann, gearrshaolach, neamhbhuan
ach tá san fíor don daonnaí, fiú.
Ba chuma liom faoin ngrian ard.
Do chasfainn uaithi le neamhaird

is chloífinn leis an doircheacht,
an amhscarnach, an clapsholas,
an aimsir mharbhánta mheirbh,
an ceo ar chnoic anuas go talamh.

Lá éigin bead im mhuisiriún
ag sá trín gcré is trín gcomhrainn throm.
Is beidh mo lámha bána lách'
i ndán don duine seang is don sách.

The Incredible Hides in Every House (Irish Writers' Centre)

ÁINE NÍ GHLINN

An Bosca Seacláide

Tar éis na sochraide thóg sí anuas an bosca coiscthe
a bhíodh riamh ar an seilf ab airde. Bhain de an ribín
bándearg seacláideach, an banda ruibéir. Agus
creathán ina láimh bhris sí an glas ar sheomra rúnda a máthar.

Seomra a bhí ag cur thar maoil le paidreacha is naoimh,
le cártaí cuimhneacháin is báis, grianghraif ó lá a pósta,
aistí gearrtha go néata as *Ireland's Own* ó chíste
Nollag go hathchúrsáil seanstocaí mar bhréagáin.

D'aithin sí bábóg a bhí roimpi ag bun na leapan maidin
Nollag, coinín bándearg cniotáilte, geansaí *fairisle* a
thug siar í chuig binse crua is na haibhneacha báistí ag
rith anuas pánaí gíoscánacha na bhfuinneog.

Thíos fúthu faoi cheilt ag patrún *His 'n Hers* — beart
grianghraf donnbhuí, báibín a raibh a súile féin aici,
cailín óg, déagóir, bean mheánaosta a d'aithin sí ach
fós nár aithin. A rún féin á scaoileadh ag na dátaí ar chúl gach uile cheann.

D'fhéach sí ar a hathair is é ag míogarnach cois tine.
Chuir ar ais an banda ruibéir, an ribín bándearg. Leag
an bosca go cúramach ar ais ar an seilf ab airde. Dúirt
paidir chiúin ar son anamacha na mbeo is na marbh.

Tostanna (Coiscéim)

GREGORY O'DONOGHUE

from *A Sofia Notebook*

Always you surprise me but never more
than when you announced "Your number is nine."
I've read enough to know this is so,
allow myself superstitious pride in it —
three times three, magical mystical number.
Nines are rare and I was only guessing
in answering "It takes one to know one."
You smiled, I smiled: two nines are eighteen;
in numerology, that is nine.
You went on "Your colours are grey and black —
you know, silvery grey with dark bits
like a feather shed by a pigeon."
I know the colours of the moon —
white, red, and black — but not my own,
perhaps they alter with moods and seasons.
Always easier to spy
colours of others — yours: silver and black…
Our days nearing their end, alone I wander
streets around the bulbous golden
onion domes of Alexandra Nevsky
searching for the right gift — find a bracelet
of silver with studs of black onyx:
silver for you are silver-tongued,
black for the storm of your dusky curls
and eyes the bluish black of ripe olives.
The jeweller, looking at me askance,
goes with my wishes: removes the tenth stud.

Southword

89

Gréagóir Ó Dúill

Faoileoir

Tiomáinim liom isteach sna cnoic, ó thuaidh,
ucht crua sin na gcnoc, gan compord ann, an carr go drogallach
ag ardú malaí, ag géilleadh d'údarás meicniúil na ngéireanna.
Tá seo le déanamh, ní bhaineann toil le scéal. Tiomáint, sea, leoga, tiomáint.

Tógaim mo shúile ar íor sin cuartha na spéire,
ar chuair na scamall troma os a chionn,
na scamaill ghormdhonna sin a bhfuil bagairt sneachta iontu
flichshneachta agus anfa doininne, pléasc toirní iontu.

Ach go tobann lingeann saor uathu, gormghlas
na spéire ollmhóire isteach, an faoileoir caol airgid
faoi sciatháin fhada, crois ag gearradh cuartha
ar éadan na firmiminte, an ciúnas beannaithe.

Crochann ar shrutha teirmeacha ag grafáil
a bhfuil ann nach dtuigim, ag foluain ar tháirní creidimh
ag áinliú ar chleití na misní, duine gan inneall,
gan talamh slán, madaidh na stoirme sna sála air

An miotal uilig ag lonrú leis faoin ghrian.

THE SHOp

90

LIAM Ó MUIRTHILE

ÁÉÍÓÚ

Ní rabhas i rang na feadóige níos mó
is dheineas scála ceoil de na gutaí fada
i rang pléascach Dermo.

 N'fheadar an b'í an phléasc
a bhlosc le slat ar aibíd
nó an riast a d'at ar bhois
ba mheasa d'aicíd,
ach ghabh lascfhórsa rois
an aeir trínn ar luas aibítreach.

Á É Í Ó Ú
dár n-imeaglú.

Á! na mianta a phléasc inár gcroí
do chuair Mhurascaill Mheicsiceo
pé acu anfa nó cúbtha chucu,
d'fhuasclaíodar sinn ó phlúchadh
comhchosach na dtriantán
is rinceamar le lúba Chúba.

Á É Í Ó Ú
dár bhfuascailt.

Lá dar chaitheamar
bailte na Mumhan
a chur isteach de láimh
ar léarscáil bhán ar an gclárdubh,
d'fhógair an Bráthair ar Fielder
Trá Lí a mharcáil is bheith amuigh.
D'fhan ina staic, balbh.
Fuair sé greadadh ó thalamh
nuair a chuir sé an baile siar
beagán ó dheas ar chuar an Bhá,
is an Bráthair ag rá
idir buillí de liú:
"Ní hea ansan ach ansan"
á aistriú soir an chuid is lú.
Chonac Bá Thrá Lí ina chruth
mar chíoch is sine le diúl
is neadaigh an Bráthair
baile cailce ar an sine
go brúidiúil.

Á É Í Ó Ú
brúidiúil.

Chaitheamar fanacht
inár gcolgsheasamh sa chlós
gan oiread is lámh ná cos
a chorraí nuair a shéid sé
an fheadóg ag an sos,
is dá mbeadh éinne fós
ag rás gan í a chlos
ghlaofaí air as a shloinne
leis an ordú pionóis:
"Go dtí an Oifig. Rith."

92

Chleachtaíos dul i bhfolach
im chorp féin ón bhfead chaol,
is phléasc neascóidí ar mo dhrom
is ceann nimhneach im ghabhal
is ba nimhní fós an neascóid
a d'fhan na blianta im cheann,
comhdhéanta de ghutaí oifigiúla.

Á É Í Ó Ú
oifigiúla.

Lá dar chaitheas féin
Locha Móra Mheiriceá
a tharraingt ar an gclárdubh
thosnaíos le Superior amuigh
i gcruth cloiginn ghadhair
mar a dheinimis le scáileanna
ar fhalla istoíche sa leaba,
is anuas ansin le Michigan
ina leadhb fhada teanga,
is ar aghaidh arís le Huron
nó gur bhagair sé orm stopadh;
"Taispeáin anois cá bhfuil Duluth."
Is nuair a dheineas go hinstinniúil
chreideas gur fíor í míorúilt.

Á É Í Ó Ú
míorúilteach.

Thugas bosca *Cadbury's Roses*
abhaile ar chúl mo rothair
mar dhuais sna cora cainte
a d'fhoghlaimíos sna leabhair,
Maidhc Bleachtaire is *Maidhc Abú*
is *Geronimo* an tíogar daonna,
is mhapálamar gnéithe aiceanta
na hÉireann mar chód géiniteach
a scaoileadh i gceol diamhair tíre,
is sheoladh long ó Valparaiso
de ghlanmheabhair i gcabhair
chun luachanna ailgéabair
a chothromú ar phár na hoíche.

Á É Í Ó Ú
dár gcothromú.

Tráthnóntaí samhraidh ar an trá
théinn ag snámh i Muir Chairbre
ar Inse an Duine sna Bahámaí
lámh le tropaicí Chloich na Coillte,
is chuala canúintí á smearadh
as na meadair ime chéanna
is leanas bóthar leáite an ime úd
ó Chorcaigh go Jamaica,
is an lá ar dhóbair don domhan
pléascadh i gcogadh núicléach
sheol an Bráthair an rang abhaile
á rá linn guí le dúthracht
go gcasfadh loingeas na Rúise
go dtiocfadh ciall chuig Kruschev,
is chonac cuntanós an Bhráthar
á chomhleá ina dhuine buartha.

Á É Í Ó Ú
dár gcomhleá.

Thug sé Cros Cheilteach isteach
lámhdhéanta as meaitseanna,
veairniseáilte is greanta
ag príosúnach i mBéal Feirste,
deartháir duine sa scoil
fé ghlas ar son na saoirse,
is chroch os cionn an chófra í
i bhfeighil Léarscáil na hÉireann;
chuimhníos ar lána sráide
ar na meaitseanna leathdhóite
ag téachtadh i sruth fola
tar éis sáthadh sa pharóiste,
is shil an Chros Cheilteach fuil
tríd an veairnis ar ár ngeograf.

Á É Í Ó Ú
dár dtéachtadh.

Lá amháin a chonac é
ag imeacht ar a rothar,
dronn ar nós an droichid air
bhuail fonn mé beannú dó
ach ghreamaigh na focail
ar an teanga bheag im scornach;
leanas é go dtí an leabharlann
mar ar sheas sé leis an ráille,
ba sheanduine leathchaoch é
ag fústráil le slabhra,
bhí fonn orm teacht i gcabhair air

go dtí go bhfaca an gotha
a bhíodh air i mbun ranga,
a theanga dingthe sna fiacla
dúbailte ag pleancadh:
"Tá milseán agam duit"
is sileadh i ngach siolla
leis an íoróin dochreidte
nuair a d'eascair as a phóca
slat chomh fada síos lena bhróga.
Bhí fonn orm a fhiafraí de
"Cad as tú?" "Cér díobh thú?
ach chuaigh díom an tuin a aimsiú
chun na focail a chur in iúl
go ndéanfadh buíochas díobh
ar scála ÁÉÍÓÚ i dtiúin.

ÁÉÍÓÚ
i dtiúin.

An Guth 3 (Coiscéim)

Catríona O'Reilly

Shortcut to Northwind

I opened it expecting something else –
the icon *Shortcut to Northwind* on a borrowed machine –
but found nothing but a white glare from an empty screen.
And after all, what was it I had wanted,
if not some afterthought of his on which I'd counted?
Its regular flicker was an electrical pulse

that made the thick glass undulate.
It reminded me of falling back on sheets,
cool sheets, with him that day in June –
at least the falling movement seemed the same,
but it was a desert I entered. What heights
those rock-needles reached I couldn't speculate.

And it was dark there though I seemed to see
by moonlight – it was moonless – a mica-glitter
or schist-shine from the wasteland all around me.
Then the wind picked up. Desert winds are bitter,
murdering with stones too small to see
that have ground each other down for centuries

and will for centuries to come. The red breath
of the desert screeched its grievance in my face
in a devil- or a lion-voice. It said:
there are worse things than the silence of the dead.
The silence that the living keep, that is a voice
of stone that will condemn. Condemn to Death —

and then it snatched me upright off my feet
and took me to a space awash with light
like diamonds thinly sprinkled on the night
or seeds sown in the furrows of darkness.
Did someone hold my hand? The air's thickness
grew, and it was without fright

I knew that I was breathing water.
It was like sliding down the surface of a jade,
like entering the glossy throats of flowers.
All the while a thin string of bubbles like tears
fell upwards from me. This rope of bead
was all that held me to the surface of the water

as I watched the sea nosing its calcined captives
like a creature, rolling them over in the sand.
A mariner's dead face wore a blue toothy smile
and his blond fronds wavered in the underwater wind.
A galley's nutmeg turned mother-of-pearl
pale in the descending light, all rippled and restive.

I could have rested there. It would have been
a salty sleep on the tongue of a mollusc,
under a nacreous canopy. But something shattered
my watery chandelier and littered
the sea's pavement with spears or narwhal-tusks
or blades of ice as hard as anything I'd seen.

And I was lifted bodily, still dripping wet,
out of the sea and into the chill of the air.
The frigid blast of his breath froze my hair
to waves of ice and froze my fingers and toes
as he wrapped me in his wings and rose
with me into the North. The stars went out

when he trailed his dirty cloak across the hills
and I saw nothing but the icicles in his beard
and eyebrows. In his pupils, back and wide,
a frosty fire burned. And he said
nothing. It was a kind of consummation, hard
and comfortless, it was exchanging one spell

in the desert for another. I dream
now of getting back to my resistless life,
to music like river-water makes in a gourd,
those plunging harmonies, myself a leaf
drunk on the surface tension and singing aloud.
Not staring at this blank and empty screen

The Sea Cabinet (Bloodaxe)

Micheál Ó Ruairc

An Cailín ar Glaodh Amach Uirthi

Cuimhním ar an gcailín
ar glaodh amach uirthi
as an rang Tíreolaíochta
ar lá breá Earraigh san anallód.
Cuimhním ar a haghaidh
ar dhath na luaithe
agus í ag fágáil an tseomra
a hatlas fágtha oscailte
ina diaidh aici
ar an mbinse adhmaid,
a peann luaidhe leagtha
anuas ar léarscáil na hEorpa
le hais na Mara Duibhe,
amhail sluasaid a bheadh caite
ar sceabha
ag béal uaighe.

Comhar

Cathal Ó Searcaigh

Do Prashant: Gúrú i gClúidíní

Ó lá do thuistí tá do theanga féin agat, a mhic ó,
faoi mar a bheadh sí leat i gcónaí, i dtaisce san méid díot a bheathaíonn,
beo síoraí, trí shaol na saol. Tá sí agat ar do bhinn féin anois agus tú
ag ainmniú laetha na seachtaine as an nua. "Dé Sú Úll, Dé Kathmandú,
Dé Búda-Buí, Dé Daidí-na-Gealaí, Dé Mamaí-na-Gréine, Dé Fonndonn,
Dé Spéirgoléir." Níl lá dá n-éiríonn nach bhfuil tú, a ghúrú na gclúidíní, ag
                                                            múnlú
d'urlabhra uaibhreach féin, ag briatharú na beatha de spalpacha reatha, a
                                        Rimbaud.
"Inniu Dé Síobsaspéir," a deir tú liom, "gheobhaidh muid scamaill i
                        dThamel, a Dhaideo."

A dhraoi an tseanchinn, a dheisbhéalaí na naoi mí déag
baineann tú as ár gcleachtadh sinn le héirim cinn
do chuid cainte agus tú ag cur d'fhírinne úraoibhinn
féin ar chiall na coitiantachta. "Tá an spéir lán d'inné,
an tsráid lán d'amárach, tá mise lá d'anois," a deir tú linn
i do ghuth glé binnbhéalach agus muid amuigh ag síneadh na ngéag
i dtráthnóna sámh na mbasár. Déanann tú do lámha a rothlú agus tig dé
bheag gaoithe ár bhfuarú. "Tá Dia te," a deir tú. "Tóg go bog é …"

Comhar

PAUL PERRY

The Gate to Mulcahy's Farm

The gate to Mulcahy's farm is crooked,
sinking into infirm soil like a ship
from the Spanish Armada if you like,
forged and felled in some dark cave

to find itself jaded with flaking eroded gilt
leaving the striations, prison-like,
shaded a coppery green. A gate without
a handle and unlike all others in any

neighbouring field with the dull sanguine
frame that swings to and fro like a hinge,
or a door itself to some other world.
No, this is no ordinary gate and there is

something majestic in its stolid refusal
to swing, something absurd even.
Perhaps this is another version of heaven,
imagine the bedroom it might once have graced,

this brass headboard, this discarded,
transported remnant of love's playground,
and look, two golden and intact globes
rest on either end, both transcendental transmitters,

receivers maybe of rough magic,
piebald love, communicating not sleep,
sleep no more, but wake, wake here
to the earth and imagine if you want

the journey of such an armature
of fecund passion, what hands gripped
these bars, what prayers were murmured
through the grate of this ribald cagery?

Imagine too the man who must have
hurled and pitched and stabbed
this frame into the ground, in a dark rain of course
after his wife had died, her passing to us unknown

though you know this
that there must have been some act
of violence within this frame-work,
some awful, regrettable pattern caught

in the form of what, wind rushing through a brass
headboard, an exclamation point to the querulous
division of fields, could we be talking border-country,
and the broken, airy, moss-eaten stone walls.

Think about when the farmer died and the farm
was sold, think about what happened the field, empty
of its cows, still with its stones and grey soil,
maybe this is Monaghan,

maybe some day it, the brass headboard
you are looking at now, will be sold
to an antiquarian in a Dublin shop,
brought there on a traveller's horse and cart,

not smelted down or disassembled, but sold
to a shop where some lady with a wallet
will buy the thing, the elegant shabbery before you
that is the gate to Mulcahy's farm. As for the bed

itself, we can speculate, let it have sunken
into the earth, or better still let the earth be the bed,
the cot, mattress and berth to this sinking headboard,
this beautiful incongruous reliquary of misplaced passion.

Winelight

GABRIEL ROSENSTOCK

Imram thar m'eolas

Glas-stócach deich mbliana d'aois a bhí ionam
Is tháinig tincéir mná chun an dorais.
Bhí réal nua agam di
Ní fhágfainn ina glac aici é:
Síos trína dhá cíoch a theastaigh uaim a chur
Go mall.
Ach bhí seál uimpi. Boladh nár aithníos.
'Cuirfidh mé síos ansin é,' a deirim.
'Ó nach tú an rógaire agam!' ar sí.
Las rud éigin ina súile.
An boladh múisiúnta sin arís. Cumhráin uile
Na hAraibe? Allas na gcapall.
Cannaí stáin os cionn bhladhmsach thine.
Caithfidh go raibh an trí scór slánaithe aici
Nó thairis.
'Cuirfidh mé síos ansin é,' ar mé
Mar bhí sí crón
Is shamhlaíos an Éigipt mhéith nó an Phuinseaib léi
Imram thar m'eolas.
'Ní chuirfidh!' ar sise.
Dhúnas an doras uirthi.

Agus cá bhfuil an réal?
Im phóca i gcónaí
Dom dhó is dom loisceadh, go mall.
An seanbholadh, ní ghlanfar é
Ná pé ní a las ina súile a bhí níos ársa ná a treibh.
Glas-stócach deich mbliana d'aois a bhí ionam.
Shamhlaíos an Éigipt mhéith nó an Phuinseaib léi.
Imram thar m'eolas.

Feasta

GERARD SMYTH

Survivors

My father knew them, the master-brewers
of Rainsford Street who watched
and learned their fathers' trade
in malt and barley, hops and yeast.
Now they are gone with all their secrets
And old ways of tossing the grain.

My father knew them, the menders
of broken shoes, the brotherhood
of men with joiner's tools and the sailors
home from the sea, who rose at noon.
Some were the forgotten of the Great War,
survivors who saw Edward Thomas's

Avenue without end. My father knew them
in their supping places, canal-barge pilots
who navigated seven locks,
the newsboys of Inchicore and Kilmainham
whose evening mantra announced
the final score, the fall of nations.

Cyphers

KELLY SULLIVAN

The Hook of Hamate

Where the Pacific meets a spit of sand
and turns it, each ashen morning,
to the south: this, the place where movement

locks into movement, where damien dogs
push their bone snouts under saltwater
and leave. The Hook of Hamate, where you walk

into the waxing tide and recite the 18 ways
of death: death by roan pony, death by alethology,
death on a slow train on the Western plains, death

in equinox, death by chorology, death on the pinions
of bridge, death quantified, death by dittology,
death under the weight of a ruined city, death

in vega, death by manatology, death
at the telling of history, death in cordovan,
death by conductivity, death at the horse latitudes,

death at temple, death in hypnology, death
where the veins cross the *tenderess membrane*,
the *lumbricals*, the dying dogs barking

one by one by one, under waves,
far off the west coast
where the Pacific drags the chaff.

Poetry Ireland Review

MATTHEW SWEENEY

Black Moon

For white he used toothpaste,
for red, blood – but only his own
that he hijacked just enough of each day.

For green he crushed basil in a little
olive oil. His yellow was egg yolk,
his black, coal dust dampened with water.

He tried several routes to blue
before stopping at the intersection
of bilberry juice and pounded bluebells.

His brown was his own, too, applied
last thing in the day before the first
Laphraoig, and the stone jug of ale.

He used no other colours, but his tone
was praised by Prince Haisal, no less,
which got him a rake of commissions

and a residency-offer in Kuwait
which he turned down. At home
the Royal Family was less generous

so he painted them all, in a series
that came to be called his brown period,

though this was strictly incorrect.

He never exhibited with other painters,
never drank with them, spoke of them —
never even spat at their work.

A cave in the Orkneys was his last dwelling
and he rode a horse to his studio.
There were no people in these paintings,

which were found piled up on one another
inside the cave, with no sign of him,
and on top was a depiction of a black moon.

London Review of Books

RICHARD TILLINGHAST

In the Parking Lot of the Muffler Shop

Between the muffler shop and the Shell station
three pines that survive where four were planted
on a strip of earth five feet across, forty long,
spill their seed cones out onto asphalt.
The pungency of eight stunted junipers
quickens the lunchtime air.

I kick indifferently among
the jetsam that has sedimented up
against the curb somebody
once painted white and then forgot about.
Dandelions take root in black sand
among filter tips, pine needles,
the snapped-off bottleneck from a longneck Bud,
rust and rubber of

manufactured parts that made cars go and stop,
things that appeased the snarl of engines
and spread the pollution out evenly.

Cool air smelling of tires and gear-box oil
exhales from the service bay of the muffler shop
as from a mountain cave.
Inside, the measured clank of heavy tools
applied with deliberation.

Three trees don't make a forest.
I sit in the shade of this reservation
between a white Cadillac and a red pine,
while some voice says to me:
Archaeologize the ordinary.
Sing songs about the late Machine Age.
Chronicle the in-between.

In the vacancy of noon,
sparrows twitter. At a distance, a phone rings.
Right here where they have spent the whole of their lives,
three pine trees stand.

Poetry London

David Wheatley

My Back Pages

I crossed the sea. Half my address book
blew away and never came back.

It's one way to weed the cabbage patch.
I never did like them all that much.

I stopped sending Christmas cards and letters.
The other half went. I never felt better.

Which left me and the takeaway man,
except when I got down to one

I wasn't so sure I made the cut
so mine was the page that I ripped out.

I'd decided I liked me less and less
I'd done my throwing out in reverse.

I was the lack that I'd always lacked.
Get rid of me and you're all welcome back.

TLS

Biographical Notes

FERGUS ALLEN: Born in London in 1921 to an Irish father and English mother. He was educated in Ireland before returning to Britain where he has lived most of his life. His first collection, *The Brown Parrots of Providencia* was published by Faber & Faber in 1993 at the age of 70. His latest book is *Gas Light & Coke* (Dedalus Press, 2006).

EAVAN BOLAND: Born in Dublin in 1944, Eavan Boland studied in Ireland, London and New York. Her first book *New Territory* was published in 1967. She has taught at Trinity College, University College Dublin and at the University of Iowa. She is currently Melvin and Bill Lane Professor in the Humanities at Stanford University, California. Her latest book *Domestic Violence (Carcanet)* is due in Spring 2007.

COLETTE BRYCE: Born in Co. Derry in 1970, Bryce won the Aldeburgh & the Eithne and Rupert Strong awards for *The Heel of Bernadette* (Picador 2000), and later won the national poetry competition, with the title poem of her second collection, *The Full Indian Rope Trick* (Picador 2004).

MAIRÉAD BYRNE: Born in Dublin in 1957. She is the author of *Nelson & The Huruburu Bird* (Wild Honey Press 2003), and three chapbooks *Vivas* (Wild Honey Press 2005), *An Educated Heart* (Palm Press 2005), and *Kalends* (Belladonna* 2005). She is an Associate Professor of English at Rhode Island School of Design.

MOYA CANNON: Born in Co. Donegal in 1956, Moya won the Brendan Behan Memorial Prize for *Oar* (Salmon, 1990) in 1991, became editor of Poetry Ireland Review in 1995 and later published *The Parchment Boat* (Gallery, 1997).

116

HARRY CLIFTON: Born in 1952, Dubliner, Harry Clifton, has lived in various parts of the world, most notably, in Africa where he worked as a teacher and in Thailand where he worked as an Aid administrator from 1980-8. He has published several collections of poetry, the most recent of which is *God in France: A Paris Sequence* 1994-98 (Metre Editions, 2003)

MICHAEL DAVITT: Poet, Michael Davitt, was born in Cork in 1950. He was educated in UCC, where he later founded the journal *Innti* in 1970, and shortly after became a key figure in a new Irish language poetry movement. He died unexpectedly in 2005.

GERALD DAWE: Belfast poet, Gerald Dawe was born in 1952. He has published the following with Gallery Press, *Lake Geneva, Morning Train, Heart of Hearts*, in 2003, 1999 and 1995, respectively. Other publications include, *Stray Dogs* and *Dark Horses*, published with Abbey Press in 2000.

JOHN F. DEANE: Deane was born on Achill Island, Co Mayo, in 1943. He founded Poetry Ireland in 1979 and was also a founder of Dedalus Press. He has published novels, short stories, poetry and literary translations. His most recent collection is *Manhandling the Deity* (Carcanet Press, 2003).

GREG DELANTY: Born in 1958, Cork poet, Greg Delanty's work is heavily influenced by his great love for his home city. His recent publication, *Collected Poems* 1986-2006 (Carcanet, 2006), is an amalgamation of his 6 previous collections, together with his most recent work, 'Aceldama', which is published for the first time in this collection. Delanty won The National Poetry Competition in 1999 and The Austin Clarke Centenary Poetry Award in 1996.

KATIE DONOVAN: Born in Wexford in 1962 to an Irish father and Canadian mother. Bloodaxe have published her three poetry collections, *Day of the Dead* (2002), *Entering the Mare* (1997), and *Watermelon Man* (1993).

TOM DUDDY: Born in Mayo, Tom now teaches philosophy at the National University of Ireland, Galway. He published a philosophical work, *A History of Irish Thought,* in 2002, and has recently published his first poetry chapbook, *The Small Hours* (2006), with Happenstance Press.

PAUL DURCAN: Born in 1944 in Westport Co. Mayo Durcan is known for his comic wit and more notably for his public denunciations of clerical and secular state institutions. His recent poetry collection is *The Art of Life* (2004).

LEONTIA FLYNN: Born in Co. Down in 1974. She won a Gregory award in 2001. Her first collection, *These Days,* was published by Jonathan Cape in 2004.

ANNE-MARIE FYFE: Born in Antrim, Anne-Marie Fyfe now lives in London. Her third collection of poetry, *The Ghost Twin,* was published by Peterloo Poets in 2005. Her previous works include, *Tickets from a Blank Window* (2002) and *Late Crossing* (1999), both of which were published by Rockingham. Her poem, 'Curaçao Dusk', was awarded first prize in the 2004 Academi Cardiff International Poetry Competition.

PEGGIE GALLAGHER: Poet and short story writer, Peggie's work has been published in Force 10, peregrine, badel (an anthology), The SHOp, Cúirt Annual, west 47 online, Cyphers, Atlantic Review, and Southword. She was awarded first prize in the Maria Edgeworth competition 2005.

SAM GARDINER: Born in Co. Armagh in 1936, Gardiner published his first collection, *Protestant Windows* with Lagan press in 2000. He won the British National Poetry Competition in 1993.

EAMON GRENNAN: Born in Dublin in 1941. Grennan's most recent poetry collection *The Quick of It* was published by Gallery in 2005. Previous poetry volumes include, *Still Life with Waterfall* (2001), for which he received the Lenore Marshall Award in 2003, and *Leopardi: Selected Poems* (1997). His poems have been awarded a number of Pushcart prizes and he received the PEN Award for Poetry in Translation.

VONA GROARKE: Born in Co. Longford, in 1964, Vona Groarke's most recent collection, *Juniper Street,* was published by Gallery in 2005. *Flight* (2002), also published by Gallery, won Groarke the Michael Hartnett Award in 2003. Other poetry prizes include the Hennessy Award, the Brendan Behan Memorial Prize, Strokestown International Poetry Award, and the Stand Magazine Poetry Prize.

KERRY HARDIE: Born in Singapore in 1951, Hardie grew up in Co. Down. Her collections published by Gallery, include *The Sky didn't Fall* (2003), *Cry for the Hot Belly* (2000) and *A Furious Place* (1996). She has also written a novel *Hannie Bennet's Winter Marriage* (HarperCollins, 2000). Her latest collection is *The Silence Came Close* (Gallery, 2006).

SEAMUS HEANEY: Born in Co. Derry, in 1939. Heaney has won the Nobel Prize for Literature. His latest collection is *District and Circle* (Faber 2006).

RITA ANN HIGGINS: Born in Galway in 1955, Higgins has published two recent collections with Bloodaxe Books, *Throw in the Vowels* (2005) and *An Awful Racket* (2001). She is also a playwright, and published *God-of-the-Hatch-Man* in 1993 and *Face Licker Come Home* in 1991.

BIDDY JENKINSON: Biddy Jenkinson (a pseudonym) was born in 1949. Her collections include *Baisteadh Gintlí* (1987); *Uiscí Beatha* (1988); *Dán na hUidhre* (1991); *An Grá Riabhach* (Baile Átha Cliath, Coiscéim, 1999); and *Rogha Dánta* (Cork University Press, 1999). Her play *Mise, Subhó agus Maccó* was produced by Aisling Ghéar, Belfast. She lives in Wicklow. Her latest collection of poems, *Oíche Bhealtaine* is published by Coiscéim. She is currently working on a collection of detective stories featuring an tAthair Pádraig Ó Duinnín as Sleuth

THOMAS KINSELLA: Born in Dublin in 1928. Kinsella has translated extensively from Irish, and his most notable translations include, *An Duanaire - Poems of the Dispossessed (1981)* and *The Táin (1969)*. He was a recipient of The Denis Devlin Memorial Award (1966, 1969, 1992) and Guggenheim Fellowships (1969, 1971). He regularly publishes his new work in limited editions under the imprint Peppercanister.

NICK LAIRD: Poet, novelist and critic, Nick Laird, was born Co. Tyrone in 1975, and has lived in both Warsaw and Boston. His first collection of poetry, *To a Fault,* was published by Faber in 2005. This same year also saw the publication of his first novel *Utterly Monkey* by Fourth Estate. He received the Eric Gregory Award in 2004 and the Cambridge Quiller-Couch Award for creative writing in 1997.

MICHAEL LONGLEY: Born in Belfast in 1939, his *Collected Poems (Cape)* was recently published in 2006. He received the Hawthornden Prize, the T. S. Eliot Prize and the Belfast Arts Award for Literature in 2000, for *The Weather in Japan (Cape)*. An earlier collection *Gorse Fires* (Cape, 1991) won him the Whitbread Poetry Award in 1991. He was more recently awarded the Queen's Gold Medal for Poetry in 2001.

JOHN MCAULIFFE: Born in Co. Kerry in 1973. Gallery published his collection, *A Better Life*, in 2002. He received the Seán Dunne National Poetry Award in 2002 and the RTÉ poet of the Future Award in 2000.

THOMAS MCCARTHY: Poet, essayist and novelist, Thomas McCarthy was born in Waterford in 1954. His first collection *The First Convention* (Dolmen) was published when he was twenty-four. He has won numerous awards including the American-Irish Foundation's Literary Award and the O'Shaughnessy Prize for Poetry. His most recent collection is *Merchant Prince* (Anvil 2005)

PETER MCDONALD: Critic and poet, Peter McDonald was born in Belfast in 1962. He has published three collections of poetry, most recent of which, *Pastorals,* was published by Carcanet in 2004. His next collection, *The House of Clay,* is due early 2007. Mc Donald won Oxford's Newdigate Prize.

DEREK MAHON Poet and translator, Derek Mahon was born in Belfast in 1941. He has worked as a teacher in America, Canada, and Ireland, and in London as a journalist, writer, reviewer and editor. Gallery published his recent poetry collections, *Harbour Lights* (2005) and *Collected Poems* (1999) *Adaptations* (June 2006, Gallery) – Translations..

DOROTHY MOLLOY: Born in Co. Mayo in 1942, Dorothy Molloy died in January 2004, the same year that her first collection, *Hare Soup (Faber)* was published. She was also an established painter and had many exhibitions of her work in Barcelona, where she lived in the 1960s and 70s. A second collection *Gethsemane Day* appeared from Faber in 2006

PATRICK MORAN: Born in Co. Tipperary. Moran's first collection *The Stubble Field* was published by Dedalus in 2001. He won the Gerald Manly Hopkins Poetry Prize in 1997.

PAUL MULDOON: Born in Co. Armagh in 1955, Paul Muldoon published his tenth collection of poetry, *Horse Latitudes (Faber)* in 2006. Other collections include, *Moy Sand and Gravel* (2002), which won the Pulitzer Prize in 2003.

GERRY MURPHY: Born in Cork in 1952, Gerry Murphy's most recent book is *End of Part One: New & Selected Poems,* published by Dedalus Press in 2006 and a translation of Polish poet, Katarzyna Borun-Jagodzinska, published by Southword Editions in 2005.

DAIRENA NÍ CHINNÉIDE: born in Kerry and raised in the Corca Dhuibhne. Her debut collection *An Trodaí agus dánta eile – The Warrior and other poems* is bilingual and published by Cló Iar-Chonnachta 2006.

NUALA NÍ DHOMHNAILL: Born in Lancashire in 1952, poet Nuala Ní Dhomhnaill, moved to Ventry, Co. Kerry at the age of 5, where she grew up speaking Irish. Her collections include *Feis* (1991) and *Féar Suaithinseach* (1984). She has also published several bilingual selections of poetry, such as *The Astrakhan Cloak* (Gallery, 1992) and *Pharoah's Daughter* (Gallery, 1990). *The Fifty Minute Mermaid* is forthcoming from Gallery.

ÁINE NÍ GHLINN: Born in Co Tipperary in 1955, poet and children's writer, Áine Ní Ghlinn has published four collections of poetry and eleven books for children. Having worked for many years as a journalist, teacher and lecturer, she now divides her time between family, writing and facilitating creative writing workshops in Gaelscoileanna.

GREGORY O' DONOGHUE: Gregory O' Donoghue was born in Cork in 1951, where he died unexpectedly in 2005. He spent many years living in Ontario. In recent years, he was poetry editor of *Southword*. His translations of Kristin Dimitrova's work *A Visit to the Clockmaker*, was published in 2005. Other works include, *Making Tracks* (Dedalus, 2001), *The Permanent Way* (Three Spires Press, 1996), and *Kicking* (Gallery Press, 1975) and posthumously *Ghost Dance* (Dedalus, 2006).

GRÉAGÓIR Ó DÚILL: Poet and critic, Gréagóir Ó Dúill, was born in Dublin in 1946 and raised in Co. Antrim. *Rogha Dánta* 1965-2001, published by Coiscéim, contains a selection of his work over a thirty year period. Other works include, a literary biography, *Samuel Ferguson: Beatha agus Saothar*, (1993) and an anthology of contemporary Ulster poetry in Irish published in 1986.

LIAM Ó MUIRTHILE: Poet, novelist and journalist, Liam Ó Muirthile, was born in Cork in 1950. A core member of the Innti group, his publications include *Dialann Bóthair* (1993, Gallery), a selection of journalistic prose: *An Peann Coitianta (1991)* and *Tine Chnámh* (1984).

CATRÍONA O' REILLY: Born in Dublin in 1973, Catríona O' Reilly grew up in Wicklow. She was awarded the Rooney prize for her first collection, *The Nowhere Birds* (Bloodaxe 2001). Her latest collection is *Sea Cabinet* (Bloodaxe 2006).

MICHEÁL Ó RUAIRC: Poet, short story writer and novelist in the Irish language. He has published four collections of poetry and six novels. He is currently working on a collection of short stories and a new poetry collection both of which are due out in 2007.

CATHAL Ó SEARCAIGH: Poet, Cathal Ó Searcaigh was born in the Donegal Gaeltacht in 1956. Collections include *Na Buachaillí Bána*, *Out in the Open* and *Homecoming (Cló Iar-Chonnachta*. His latest collection of poems, *Aingeal on tSolais* is due in 2007.

PAUL PERRY: Born in Dublin in 1972. He has published two collections *The Drowning of the Saints* (Salmon, 2003) and *The Orchid Keeper* (Dedalus, 2006). He has won the Hennessy New Irish Writer of the Year Award and The Listowel Prize for Poetry. He has also had a poem published in *The Best of American Poetry* anthology series.

GABRIEL ROSENSTOCK: Poet and translator, Gabriel Rosenstock was born in Limerick in 1949. He mainly writes in Irish and is assistant editor of An Gúm. His most recent collections include, *Rogha Dánta / Selected Poems*, published by Cló Iar-Chonnachta in 2005 and *Krisnmurphy Ambaist*, which was published by Coiscéim in 2004. Rosenstock's translations into the Irish language include the works of Yeats, *Byzantium* (1991) and Heaney, *Conlán* (1989), amongst many others.

GERARD SMYTH: Born in Dublin in 1951, he has published five collections to date. His most recent *A New Tenancy* (2004) and *Daytime Sleeper* (2002) were published by Dedalus. The latter was translated and published in Romania. He works as an editor for the Irish Times.

KELLY SULLIVAN: Born in Lancaster County, Pennsylvania, in 1979. She graduated from Skidmore College (Saratoga Springs, New York) in 2002, and was awarded a Fulbright Scholarship to study in Ireland in 2002/2003. Her novel *Winter Bayou* was published by Lilliput in 2004. She lives in Dublin.

MATTHEW SWEENEY: Poet and novelist, Mathew Sweeney was born in Co. Donegal in 1952. He has also written poetry and novels for children. His latest collection is *Sanctuary* (Cape, 2004) He received the Arts Council Writers' Award in 1999 and the Cholmondeley Award in 1987.

RICHARD TILLINGHAST: Born 1940 in Memphis Tennessee. He has published seven collections of poetry as well as a critical memoir on Robert Lowell. *Today in the Café Trieste*, a selection from his first five books was published by Salmon in 2001. He divides his time between America and Ireland where he has a home.

DAVID WHEATLEY: Poet, David Wheatley, was born in Dublin in 1970. He has published three collections with the Gallery Press the most recent being *Mocker* (2006). Wheatley was awarded the Rooney prize for Irish literature in 1998 and the Friends Provident National Poetry Competition in 1994.

ACKNOWLEDGEMENTS

The publishers would like to thank Colm and Maurice for their diligence in preparing this volume. We would also like to thank Paul Lenehan of Poetry Ireland for his invaluable assistance. Thanks are also due to the editors of many of the journals and book presses where the poems first appeared as mentioned at the end of each poem and for the generosity of those editors who supplied us with the source materials required to make the selection.

A sincere attempt has been made to locate all copyright holders before publication. Unless otherwise stated, copyright to the poems is held by the individual poets.

Fergus Allen: "Alessandro Moreschi, Castrato" reprinted by permission of the *Dedalus Press.*
Evan Boland: "And Soul" reprinted by permission of the poet.
Colette Bryce: "Self-portrait (In the Dark with Cigarette)" reprinted by permission of the poet.
Mairéad Byrne: "I Went to the Doctor" reprinted by permission of the poet.
Moya Cannon: "The Train" reprinted by permission of the poet.
Harry Clifton: "McCrystal's" reprinted by permission of the poet.
Michael Davitt: "Déirc" reprinted by permission of Moira Sweeney who retains copyright.
Gerald Dawe: "Points West" reprinted by permission of the poet.
John F. Deane: "Towards a Conversion" reprinted by permission of the poet.
Greg Delanty: "Aceldama" reprinted by permission of *Carcanet.*
Katie Donovan: "Buying a Body" reprinted by permission of the poet.
Tom Duddy: "Side Street" reprinted by permission of the poet.
Paul Durcan: "Let the Hierarchy Go Play Croquet in Honolulu" reprinted by permission of the poet.